THE STORY OF
NEWBURY

David Peacock

COUNTRYSIDE BOOKS

NEWBURY BERKSHIRE

First published 2011
© David Peacock 2011

COUNTRYSIDE BOOKS
3 Catherine Road
Newbury, Berkshire

To view our complete range of books,
please visit us at
www.countrysidebooks.co.uk

ISBN 978 1 84674 273 6

To Pam

The cover painting shows Newbury bridge c1855,
by W. Henry Gore (local collection)

Produced through MRM Associates Ltd., Reading
Typeset by CJWT Solutions, St Helens
Printed by Information Press

Contents

Introduction

The Story of Newbury comes with a completely new text, although it follows in the tradition of previous books with the same title. It attempts to describe the history of Newbury from the primitive flint tools found at Wash Common across thousands of years to the opening of the Parkway shopping centre. With additional information and updating, it was decided to focus more on the town of Newbury. At times this has meant leaving out topics which are historically important, but better covered elsewhere (for example in a history of Thatcham or Hungerford).

I have tried to present a taste of Newbury's fascinating history, with its rich variety, and also to draw attention to buildings and other reminders of its past. To me, there is so much which ought to be more widely known. For example, Donnington Castle has a history which is intriguing but largely untold. And I do feel that if John Winchcombe had lived in another town, he would have become an established figure in British (i.e. *national*) history. In a book of this size it is not possible to write a full and detailed history covering everything, even by restricting the subject-matter largely to the town of Newbury. There is much I have left out and, in the end, the selection was a matter of my personal choice.

Much original research has gone into this book, and that accounts for some of the changes in interpretation when compared with previous histories. As far as possible, every piece of information has been checked but if readers are aware of any errors, I would welcome information so that corrections, if appropriate, can be made in any future reprint.

David Peacock

Acknowledgements

The idea for a simple, readable history of Newbury came about in the 1970s as a result of the popularity of the former Borough Guide, with its description of Newbury's history and its buildings, written by local historian R. Neville Hadcock. A book with Hadcock's text appeared in 1979 as *The Story of Newbury*, published by Countryside Books. This was later revised and expanded, in editions by Cecilia Millson and Tony Higgott.

The publishers are grateful to photographers and others who have provided illustrations for this new book, including the *Newbury Weekly News* and Oxford Archaeology. They are also grateful to Mrs Sue Hopson who has made several images available from her collection.

Very many thanks to Tony Higgott for his valuable suggestions, and the care and patience he has shown. Thanks to Dave and the Dixon family for their suggestions and my thanks also to Nicholas Battle, Paula Leigh and all the team at Countryside Books.

I would like to record my appreciation to all of these, to others who have helped, and to everyone who has given encouragement and support over the years.

Chapter 1

Before Newbury

The earliest signs of man to be found in the Newbury area are the crude flint tools which were used during the Old Stone Age, up to 250,000 years ago. Among these are the multi-purpose hand-axes found in the gravelly soils which cover the higher ground, such as the six found at Wash Common and others discovered among gravels along the Kennet Valley. The Old Stone Age was a time of massive changes in climate which included several Ice Ages. No evidence of human habitation has survived locally, but mammoth tusks and teeth have been found, while evidence of warmer periods includes the bones of a hippopotamus, found at Shaw when the present A339 was being built.

The Kennet Valley from Hungerford to Woolhampton is one of the most important lowland areas in England for finds from the Middle Stone Age, or Mesolithic period, which lasted until about 4,000 BC. Archaeologists have uncovered a number of tool-making sites, where shaped thin blades were removed from large chunks of flint, and smaller tools made from many of the blades. These included microliths, which were tiny pointed flints used for arrow-heads, harpoons and other items. A major site off Lower Way in Thatcham was excavated in 1921, and finds uncovered nearby about 40 years later were dated to 10,000 years ago.

In Newbury, several sites excavated in the Faraday Road area tell the story of prehistoric hunting parties regularly visiting the area, travelling along the rivers, catching and roasting young wild boar, and eating hazelnuts. To the west of Newbury some sites have produced thousands of waste flints, the debris from a process which saw most of the finished products taken out of the area. Many of the local sites were visited year after year for long periods. At Thatcham bone and antler hammers were found for shaping the flint. When the boating pond was made in Victoria Park, a tranchet axe (a flint tool with a shape similar to a pick-axe head) was found.

The following New Stone Age or Neolithic period was the time when population became more settled, and agriculture became widespread. The most visible remains are long barrows, substantial burial mounds with chambers at one end for the interment of bones. The nearest good example is Wayland's Smithy (on the Ridgeway north of Lambourn), but there were several others on the Berkshire and North Hampshire downs, including the long barrow above Inkpen with Combe Gibbet staked through its centre. The Ridgeway itself, now a long-distance footpath, probably dates from this period. A Neolithic saddle quern – a stone on which corn was ground – was found at Newtown Common, a number of stone axe-heads from the period have been found in the area, and this period left the first fragments of pottery.

Burial mounds from the Bronze Age can be found scattered across the Newbury area, alone or grouped in cemeteries, such as those near Lambourn or below Beacon Hill. Some of these covered a central funeral pyre, and many contain cremation burials. Distinctive bronze daggers and other items identify them as the burying places of the Wessex Culture, centred on Wiltshire. There is a cluster of these mounds or barrows at Wash Common. Two are now visible on the recreation ground (where a third was still visible in the 1930s). Another barrow lies on the edge of the

In Faraday Road, Stone Age (mesolithic) hunters roasted wild boar at their camp. (© Wessex Archaeology)

woods, and used to be a landmark on the parish boundary between Newbury and Enborne. There is a fourth Bronze Age feature, more unusually shaped, nearby in the woods.

For many years the barrows were described as the burial places of those who died in the First Battle of Newbury, and the two on the recreation ground still carry stone tablets to that effect. It is highly likely that some of the debris from the battle has been mixed into their earth. But archaeologists now agree in describing them as a Bronze Age cemetery. The circular feature in the woods, which has been described as a small 'henge' or as a disc barrow, is now officially described as a 'ring mound'. Also at Wash Common, two stone hammers and a bronze axe were found; and during the construction of Conifer Crest two baked clay weights from a weaving loom were discovered which have been identified as Bronze Age.

For centuries a long bank of earth, known as Bury's Bank, was a prominent feature on Greenham Common. Part of this was described in 1945 as 1.2 metres (4 ft) high and 9 metres (30 ft) wide, running alongside a ditch which was also 9 metres wide. This bank ran from the centre of

This picture taken from the interpretation panel at Wash Common shows the Bronze Age burial mounds (barrows).

the Common north to the area near the Golf Club, and is all that survived in living memory. However, an 18th century map shows that Bury's Bank originally stretched north-south across the whole of the high ground of the Common, descending on both sides. To the south it crossed the course of the present Basingstoke Road, almost reaching the River Enborne. Earthworks can be very difficult to date, but this style of earthwork appears to be a Bronze Age boundary bank known as a 'cross-ridge dyke'. Despite the amount of work needed to create them, they are often explained as ranch boundaries. All trace of it was removed by the Greenham Common airfield.

The first local hillforts, such as Uffington Castle, were built at the end of the Bronze Age. More followed, with surviving examples including those at Hermitage and on the edge of Snelsmore, and evidence of another to the north of Thatcham. There are also important hillforts to the south of Newbury at Ladle Hill and Beacon Hill, the latter controlling the gap through the Downs now occupied by the A34. The hillforts were occupied throughout the Iron Age, not always continuously.

The Iron Age in Britain started with the introduction of iron, which has been dated to about 700 or 800 BC. However, a site just outside Thatcham is helping to change that, because excavation has shown that ironworking was taking place there in the 10th century BC. The site lies off Hartshill Road, between Thatcham and Bucklebury. Archaeologists uncovered the remains of a round-house, a work area for a blacksmith, and a second round-house where a large number of tiny fragments of iron provided evidence of a workshop for high-temperature iron-working. Despite these finds, pottery and other evidence from the site is seen as Bronze Age, supporting the early date.

A fine early Iron Age bronze brooch was found at Northcroft, and evidence of round-houses, pottery fragments and other signs of occupation have been found in the Newbury and Thatcham area (including at Dunston Park on the east side of Thatcham, where post-holes provided evidence for a round-house 11 metres across).

In the late Iron Age, Newbury was part of the tribal area of the Atrebates. This was one of the tribes from northern France known as the Belgae, and they established nearby Silchester in the 1st century BC. They issued coins, sometimes found by metal-detectors, and a gold coin from this period (showing a horse with three tails) was found at Wash Common. Their kings'

Pottery from a cremation burial almost 2,000 years old, discovered while building the West Berkshire Community Hospital. (© Oxford Archaeology)

names are known, and these are the earliest personal names with a direct association to the Newbury area. Agriculture flourished. In the decades leading up to the arrival of the Romans, life in the Newbury area became increasingly sophisticated, with a lifestyle anticipating Roman Britain.

Two cremation burials from this period were found during the construction of the West Berkshire Community Hospital, close to the A4 between Newbury and Thatcham. In one, a bag of cremated bones was placed in the centre of a pit, surrounded by nine separate items of wheel-turned pottery. These included a platter on which a knife had been placed. With the bones were three brooches, at least one of which was on the body at the time it was cremated.

Newbury in the Roman period

The nearest substantial Roman settlement to Newbury was Calleva, now Silchester. One major road travelled from London to Calleva and from there crossed the Newbury area, heading towards Cirencester and Gloucester. It left Calleva through a double-arched gateway, and as part of the major road network it could be considered a motorway of its day.

For centuries it was thought that this road stayed south of the River Kennet until it reached Newbury, crossing Crookham and Greenham Commons before descending via Pyle Hill. From the early 20th century, the understanding has been instead that the road crosses the Kennet at Colthrop, continuing until it joined the line of the Bath Road in Thatcham. Much evidence of Roman occupation has been found close to the Bath Road between Northfield Road and Henwick Lane, including the Roman Way area, which used to be known as Thatcham Newtown. Little evidence of buildings was uncovered, but finds included a decorated pewter flagon and other pewter items, the whereabouts of which are currently not known. The road passed north of Newbury town centre, crossing from Shaw to Speen until it joined up with the line of the modern B4000, which follows the Roman road for much of its length. Modern archaeological discoveries have supported this as the major route, although it leaves open the routes of less significant Roman roads in the area. The excavations for the A34 Newbury bypass cut through the line of the Roman road. Confirming its location would have helped to prove the exact route crossing Newbury; but the archaeologists apparently found no evidence for it.

To the north-west of Newbury, in the Wickham area, the major road forked, with one road heading west towards Avebury and on to Bath, while the other continued north-west towards Baydon and Gloucester. Details of the road network survive from the Roman period and show that there was a settlement called Spinae (dative 'Spinis') in the Newbury area. However, the details include an error in calculating the Roman miles, so that its position is uncertain. For centuries it was thought to be at Speen, or Woodspeen, mainly because of the similarity of the names: but so far there have been no archaeological discoveries to support this. The Roman finds at Thatcham led some to conclude that Spinae was there. The indications are that Spinae was between Thatcham and Wickham, definitely in the Newbury area, but the location is still unknown.

An extensive Roman cemetery in Newbury was discovered in the Victorian period. The cemetery was found close to the modern Sainsbury's supermarket, near the railway on the edge of Newbury Goods Yard. About 100 graves were uncovered, along with burnt bones and ash showing that additional cremations were also there. The find was made in 1856, when workmen were digging gravel on the eastern side of the site (i.e. near the Gordon Road area), and there was no professional archaeological investigation. However, local antiquaries were interested

An amphora, bowls and a glass flask were among the items discovered in 1856 from the Roman cemetery near Sainsbury's.

and some details were reported. On the first day they found the complete remains of three people; by the end of the week they had discovered the remains of six more skeletons, with no trace of a coffin or coffin nails for any of them. All nine were adults, with eight of them buried six feet deep, and one three feet down. Two weeks later nearly 100 graves had been found. The skeletons lay in black earth within the gravel, with bodies orientated north-south instead of east-west (which would be the normal orientation for a Christian burial).

An extensive array of finds was uncovered with them, and some of these have survived. Collectors descended on the site to acquire genuine Roman artefacts, and no record was taken. The collectors were looking for complete items, with little interest in the abundance of (for example) pottery fragments, which would now provide considerable information about the cemetery and the lives of the people buried there. In addition, there was no local museum at that time, and the finds were scattered, sometimes passing through various hands before Newbury Museum managed to acquire some of them in 1916. So the surviving finds represent only a fraction of the goods interred in the cemetery.

Even so, some of the finds are impressive. They include a glass bottle or phial, of a type normally known as an *unguentaria*. This stands 15.9 cm (6¼ inches) high, and although it is the kind of bottle which would have held Roman perfumes or ointments, in this case it appears to have contained some kind of medicine. The letters 'S P S' appear on the bottom of the bottle, along with a figure of Aesculapius and a serpent. Aesculapius was the Roman god of medicine, whose symbol is a staff with a snake entwined around it. Also found was another glass phial, of a similar shape, but this time only 9.5 cm (3¾ inches) high. Like the larger example, it dates from the 2nd century AD. Bearing in mind the way the cemetery was found, and the lack of delicacy in the way the finds were treated, it is impressive that these glass objects survived at all.

Among the pottery were imported items made in Gaul and other parts of the Roman Empire. These included three cups in an orangy-red finish, probably from the 1st century AD. Two of these feature the maker's stamp, different potters both based in La Graufesenque, in southern Gaul. Two bowls or *patera*, with the same finish, show maker's stamps for different potters, both this time from Rheinzabern in south-west Germany. All of these were displayed for decades in Newbury Museum, now known as West Berkshire Museum, but with no accompanying information to identify the link with the Newbury cemetery.

Other finds included an amphora, with a rounded or globe-shaped body, a narrow neck and two handles. This was 33 cm (13 in.) high, 71 cm (28 in.) in circumference, and a pale ash colour. And there were various other urns and bowls, most in perfect condition. One black urn still contained burnt bones. West Berkshire Museum also has a bronze Roman lamp, said to have been found in Newbury in 1856, which means that it is also likely to have come from this cemetery.

Much of the pottery has been generally described as Samian, but there has been no comprehensive modern reassessment of the finds, in spite of the size and importance of the cemetery. Nor is it clear whether the whole of the cemetery was uncovered. Excavation has shown there is no more to be found underneath Sainsburys and SCATS, so if the cemetery does continue it is into the higher ground on which the houses of Gordon Road stand, or (on the opposite side of the railway) under the north end of Jubilee Road and adjacent housing.

In the Roman period it was common practice for a cemetery to be sited alongside roads leaving a town or settlement. In spite of the size of the Newbury cemetery, so far no evidence has been found of the settlement to which it relates; but to date no serious investigation has taken place.

On the opposite side of Newbury town centre was another Roman cemetery, smaller and as far as is known, consisting only of cremation burials. This was discovered in 1907 in a field on the south side of Enborne Road, now the Kingsbridge Road and Salcombe Road area. A large number of cremation urns were reported at the time, in rows, nearly parallel to the Enborne Road at a depth of about 18 inches. All of these were wheel-turned, and of a blue-black colour. Several of the urns had a diameter of about 25 cm (10 inches); some were plain and others more ornate.

On this site, there were lengths of Roman wall, made from flint with some blocks of chalk, clay roof and floor tiles, and parts of the flues for an underfloor heating system (hypocaust). There were also pieces of internal plasterwork, showing that it had been painted. This is now described as a likely villa site.

There was no evidence of mosaics, but there was a range of pottery, including jars, jugs and bottles. A well on the site was found to contain fragments of earthenware, mainly grey, and kitchen mortars. One Roman coin was also found, but in poor condition and unreadable.

Several more Roman sites to the west of Newbury were located during the construction of the A34 bypass. These included a site between Enborne Road and the railway, occupied in the late 3rd and 4th centuries. This included a substantial building of tile, flint and stone, and was probably an extensive farmstead. Instead of being excavated, this was largely buried under the bypass embankment in order to preserve it. Another part of the same site produced pottery from close to the time of the Roman Conquest. Roman features were also discovered at Elmore Plantation, Speen, suggesting a Roman farmstead there, and there was also a Roman farmstead near Bagnor.

The Anglo-Saxon period

Another cemetery sheds some light on the way life changed in the Newbury area after the nominal end of the Roman period in AD 410. This is the Anglo-Saxon cemetery at East Shefford in the Lambourn valley. Even though many items from this cemetery are now in the British Museum (including an impressive pair of the gold brooches which have been on the British Museum's website for years), it is hardly known among local residents.

The cemetery was first discovered in 1889. There was no comprehensive archaeological report, but at least 46 graves were uncovered at that time. Further excavation before the First World War took the total to at least 74. The cemetery dates from the 5th and 6th centuries, the pre-Christian era which has often been described as the 'Dark Ages'. Those buried were male and female, adults and children.

Interred with the bodies were a wide range of Saxon artefacts such as brooches, knives, pottery and glassware, and the discovery was seen as important enough to feature in *The Times* newspaper.

Some of the finds suggest how society was changing locally. The evidence is of continuity through from the Roman period. This is not one society displacing another by warfare; it is a merging of cultures: a brooch that takes a Roman detail and puts it in a Saxon setting; and Roman coins, having lost their practical use, being treated as jewellery. The whole collection includes a multitude of small Saxon knives, several well-preserved pieces of Saxon pottery, and a number of bead necklaces. Brooches are cross-shaped, disc-shaped and saucer-shaped, many of them gilded and some carrying zoomorphic designs, with animals emerging from abstract patterns.

But the most impressive items are those made of glass. These include fragments of a delicately-made bowl, and three glass drinking beakers in the shape of ice-cream cones. Two of these 'cone beakers' have a thin line of spiral glass decoration running down the cone. In addition, there was another beaker with strange claw-shaped glass decorations attached to the cone. This seems to be a continuation of a Roman style of glass-making, probably imported into England, but after the recognised end of the Roman period. One of the beakers used to be on display in Newbury Museum, but is in need of professional restoration before it can be displayed again.

In spite of their importance, the glass finds are not well known. One author has suggested that they imply prosperity at East Shefford in the immediately post-Roman period. He wrote that to find five glass vessels at any site in England outside Kent is unusual at this time. A number of the finds from East Shefford have formed part of displays in the British Museum, in the same gallery which includes the Sutton Hoo treasure. So far, there has been no evidence of the Saxon settlement which the cemetery served.

Most of the villages in the area were created and named during the Anglo-Saxon period, with a tendency to pick sites along streams or rivers for the water supply and to power corn mills. Village names containing the elements 'ham-', '-stead', and '-ton' provide many examples. Thatcham probably takes the first part of its name from the Anglo-Saxon for 'thatch', although it has been suggested that it comes from a person's name, 'Tac' or 'Tace'. Some place-names have very specific meanings. The man responsible for raising an army in a county in the Anglo-Saxon period was the earldorman, a title later abbreviated to Earl. In Anglo-Saxon Berkshire, the earldorman was based at 'earldorman's/ton', the original form of the name of Aldermaston.

For most of the Anglo-Saxon period Berkshire was part of the Kingdom of Wessex, and it was during this period that the name of the county emerged. In spite of claims that the system of shires or counties in Wessex was created by Alfred the Great, it is clear that their origins go back further. Like other Wessex shires, Berkshire, as an administrative unit, existed before the end of the 8th century. Its earliest form appears to be as 'Berroc/scire', and authorities on the Anglo-Saxon language (Old English) have explained the 'Berroc' element as identifying a large wood from which the county received its name. The location of the wood is unclear, but some medieval evidence points to it running along the Berkshire Downs (also known now as the North Wessex Downs); and all evidence points to it being in the south-western third of the historic county, i.e. part of the Newbury area.

Each county was divided into administrative areas known as 'Hundreds'. Newbury was in Thatcham Hundred, along with Bagnor, Brimpton, Crookham, Curridge, Donnington, Greenham, Midgham, Shaw, Speen, Wasing and Thatcham itself. This reflected the relative importance at that time of Thatcham, and the relative insignificance of the area which was still to become Newbury.

In the period before the Norman Conquest, however, the area which is now called Newbury was called 'Ulvritone' instead. This name (or 'Uluritone', as 'u' and 'v' were interchangeable) appears in an abbreviated form in the Domesday Book. Newbury's lack of importance in the pre-Conquest period is emphasized by the fact that no contemporary trace of Newbury or 'Ulvritone' survives other than that recorded in the Domesday Book. There it is listed as being held from King Edward the Confessor by Wulfward ('Uluuard'), who was not a prominent member of Saxon society. Contemporary records show that places such as Thatcham, Lambourn, Kintbury and even Welford and Brimpton were all of importance during the Saxon era, but Newbury became significant only after the Conquest.

Chapter 2

The Middle Ages: New Town to Royal Rebellion

Newbury came into existence shortly after the Norman Conquest. Enough detail appears in the Domesday Book of 1086 to suggest that the town was effectively a Norman creation, a new town or borough created by its new lord. Before the Conquest and shortly afterwards it was not worth much, but by 1086 its value had risen substantially, showing that it had expanded rapidly.

By 1086, the population was roughly 100. Domesday Book lists 11 high-status peasants or villeins, with 11 more peasants of lower status. These 22 would have been heads of households, and a realistic figure for total population would be between four and five times as great. In contrast to the number of households, the figure for properties or sites ('haga') in 1086 is given as 51.

The Norman lord of the manor, effectively owning Newbury at the time of the Domesday Book, was Arnulf de Hesdin (written as 'Ernulf de Hesding' in the survey). He took his title from the area of Hesdin in France, inland from Calais, and he was one of a number of people from outside Normandy who joined up with William the Conqueror for the invasion of England. This was not Arnulf de Hesdin's only English manor; his main concentration of property and his base was at Chipping Norton, north-west of Oxford. Newbury was simply one of the sources of his income.

Domesday Book, which took several years to compile, gives some additional information about the expanding settlement. The survey lists two mills, which were corn mills. In many cases mills continued to occupy the same sites for centuries, and the likely Domesday sites are at Town Mills (now occupied by flats) and further west on the island site across the swing bridge at West Mills. Newbury had agricultural land for 12 ploughs, each plough having its own team of oxen. There were also 27 acres of meadow, and woodland taxed at 25 pigs.

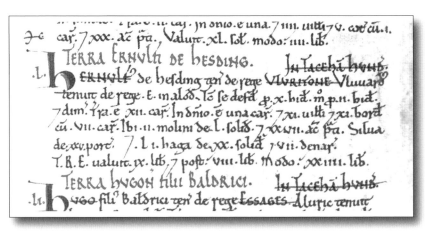

The Domesday entry for Newbury.

The name 'Newbury' does not appear in the Domesday Book, where it is listed as 'Ulvritone' instead. The renaming took place during the years while the Domesday Book was being compiled. The first reference to Newbury by that name dates from about 1080. The introduction of the new name is seen as recognition of the change in status, with its literal meaning: 'new town'.

No church in Newbury appears in the Domesday Book, although a number of others are listed in the surrounding area. Surviving documents show that the parish church of St Nicolas at Newbury was built in the two decades after the Conquest, during the time that the Domesday Book was being compiled, and at about the same date as the introduction of the new name. No visible remains of this Norman building now survive, as the church was comprehensively rebuilt in the Tudor period.

Like most churches, there were changes to the building and its uses as the Middle Ages progressed, so that in the 15th century the medieval church had several additional chapels with their own altars. Legacies to the church included property left by Robert Bullock in the 14th century, to pay for a priest to say prayers at the altar of the Blessed Virgin Mary, every day, forever. The priest would pray for the soul of Bullock, his family, and Newbury parishioners.

Newbury was caught up in the events of the 12th-century civil war. A castle at Newbury was besieged in 1152 by forces led by King Stephen himself. This was not Donnington Castle, which would not be erected for more than two centuries: it is a reference to Newbury Castle, about which very little is known. This castle in a stylised form, with stone walls and towers, later became part of the coat of arms of the Borough of Newbury, one version of which can be seen over the entrance to the Corn Exchange. However, as a Norman castle it could have been made of stone or it could have been a motte-and-bailey structure, which would be less dramatic and leave less substantial remains. The civil war ended the year after the Newbury siege, with a treaty signed at Wallingford.

The rights to hold markets and fairs were valuable properties in the Middle Ages, in Newbury as elsewhere, with the benefit from tolls and fees going to the Lord of the Manor unless another body was specified. There is no clear date for the start of Newbury Market. Cheap Street takes its name from 'chepe', the Old English or Anglo-Saxon for market, but there is no evidence of it in the Saxon period and bearing in mind the relative insignificance of Newbury at that time it seems unlikely. It is more likely to have started with the new town, and the evidence points to it beginning in the Norman period. This is one inference to be drawn from a 12th-century conflict between Newbury and Thatcham, which suggests that the two markets were already competing. About 1160 Newbury people attacked their nearby rival, and in response a Charter of King Henry II forbade the men of Newbury from doing any injury to the market at Thatcham. Tolls from the market are frequently mentioned among documents recording the assets of each Lord of the Manor, at the time of his death. In 1205 the toll from Newbury market is recorded as £8.

Even in the Middle Ages, Newbury Market seems to have taken place regularly on Thursdays and Saturdays but its status was fully recognized only with the creation of the Borough of Newbury during the Tudor period. A market cross survived on the southern side of the Market Place into the 19th century.

The earliest fair documented for Newbury was an annual two-day fair on 24 and 25 August which was granted in 1215 (the year of Magna Carta) by King John. The income from this fair, on St Bartholomew's Day and the day following, went to St Bartholomew's Hospital in Newtown Road. By the end of the 16th century this had been taken over by the town or borough, and was one of at least four Newbury fairs held on a regular basis, which also included one each on the Annunciation (25 March), the Nativity of St John the Baptist (24 June) and the Feast of St Simon and St Jude (28 October).

Newbury's Market Cross, which survived into the 19th century. This is part of a picture by Thomas Rowlandson (1756–1827).

However, other fairs were also granted at different periods. Under King Edward IV, the rights were granted to hold two more fairs in Newbury, with much of the income kept by the Crown. These were on the Eve of Corpus Christi (the Wednesday following the eighth Sunday after Easter), and the Eve of the Nativity of St John the Baptist (23 June).

The continued success of the market and more particularly the fairs was partly due to Newbury's position on the medieval road network. It lay on the important north-south road running from the thriving port of Southampton, passing through the major city of Winchester, and arriving in Newbury from Newtown and Sandleford along Old Newtown Road. The road then continued north to medieval Oxford.

Less important in the Middle Ages but still significant was the road running east-west between London to Bristol, both major ports. This came in along London Road to Speenhamland (the area around the Clock Tower, which was then part of Speen rather than Newbury). It continued west along what is now the Old Bath Road (formerly Speen Hill).

Other roads left Newbury for Wantage, the Vale of the White Horse, and on to the Cotswolds; for Streatley, and a historic crossing of the Thames; for Basing (leaving along Greenham Road/Pyle Hill before crossing Greenham Common towards not only Old Basing and Basingstoke, but also Chichester and the medieval port of Shoreham, near Brighton); and for Salisbury via Andover.

Near the bottom of the hill leading towards Andover, occupying land between Argyle Road and Newtown Road was St Bartholomew's Hospital, a combination of religious institution and hospital. No date has been established for its foundation, but it is likely to be shortly before 1200. In July 1215, the year of Magna Carta, it received a grant from King John. This gave St Bartholomew's Hospital the right to hold a fair on St Bartholomew's Day (24 August) and the following day. The right to hold a fair was essentially a right to collect an income in the form of tolls and other fees, and the fair was established just east of the hospital, in nearby Fair Close.

Over the years St Bartholomew's Hospital amassed wealth in the form of land, mainly in and around Newbury. It continued its combined activities until the Tudor period, when its role was radically changed. Of the medieval buildings, only one now survives: part of the Litten Chapel, with its flint walls, much altered. A small section of the adjacent cemetery, on the north side of the chapel, was excavated in 2004. The first burials

The Litten, at the junction of Newtown Road and Pound Street, as it looked in the early 19th century.

uncovered were from the 13th century, laid out in neat rows, and other burials followed, crowded in phases into the same ground, with the use of the cemetery ending by the middle of the 16th century. The excavation uncovered 59 graves, stretching out to the edge of Pound Street, and many additional bones. An analysis of the skeletons confirmed evidence for St Bartholomew's medieval role as a hospital in the modern sense.

The hospital's chapel had particular importance for midwifery and childbirth, and was associated with St Leonard. One 16th-century witness described the custom: 'Always on St. Leonard's Day all the wives of Newbury, with the midwife, were accustomed to offer in the Chapel … to an image there in the said church called St Leonard, certain oblations, that is to say, candles and other things …'.

St Bartholomew's Hospital is also the body out of which St Bartholomew's School emerged in the early Tudor period (before 1548). It was only for boys and it remained at the Litten for centuries.

Another hospital, dedicated to St Mary Magdalene and for women with leprosy, is mentioned in 1232, during Henry III's reign. Over a century later in 1375 there is a reference to a hospital of sisters known as the House of Blessed Mary, and in 1604 the St Mary's Almshouses, for six poor women, were described as 'ancient'. All three references may be to the same institution, its name and function evolving as centuries passed. The almshouses mentioned in 1604, in Cheap Street, continued in use until 1967 (and were replaced by Mill Reef House).

Sandleford Priory

Around 1200 a priory for Augustinian monks was established at Sandleford. It was set up by Geoffrey, Count of Perche, an active Crusader who had fought beside his father at the Siege of Acre. Geoffrey de Perche owned large areas of land in France, and married King Richard's niece. He died in France, taken ill while planning another expedition to the Holy Land. It was in the ten years before his death in 1202 that he and his wife established the priory at Sandleford. A monument of a knight, thought to be either Geoffrey or his son Thomas, survived in the priory's chapel until at least the 18th century. It represented the knight in mail, lying down with his legs crossed, with a large shield on one arm while the other was drawing a sword.

The priory itself was small, with only a handful of Augustinian monks, known as Austin Canons, who followed a rule more flexible than those of cloistered monks. Geoffrey ensured that Sandleford Priory was given a secure income right from the start. As well as receiving his land at Sandleford, it was given permission to build a mill on the River Enborne and was allocated a monthly income from Town Mills, on the Kennet in Newbury.

Additional grants of land were made later, and the priory's wealth steadily grew. It owned considerable property in the southern half of Newbury, and stretching across from the Argyle Road/Andover Road area into Enborne, as well as further afield. At one time or another, the priory drew its income from Newbury, Enborne, Speen, Greenham, Midgham, Beenham, Aldworth, Wallingford, West Ilsley, East Garston, Kingsclere and Pamber. And as some mark of its status, the priory is said to have received two royal visits – from Henry II in 1234 and from Edward II in 1320.

But it does not appear to have been a thriving concern. In 1274 there were only three monks at the priory, who were described as 'imperfectly observing their rule' in spite of – or perhaps because of – an income of £100 a year. And from then until 1320 they do not appear to have chosen a prior to take charge. They were often slow to pay their debts.

Its later history features the story of Prior Simon Dam, who was dismissed from office in 1440. He seems to have fallen for 'Thomasia of the Black Brows' who came from London. He had visited the capital with her several times, but his problems started when two local people discovered that she was living with him at the priory. He tried to bribe them to keep quiet by offering them 20 shillings and eight cartloads of faggots, but they turned it down and informed on him. The Bishop of Salisbury launched an inquiry and found that Simon had also pawned the priory's chalice, was not maintaining the building, and was letting off one of its fields near East Garston at a third of its real value. The Prior was publicly deposed in St Nicolas' church in Newbury, and his position was given to a canon from Bisham Abbey.

Far from turning over a new leaf the priory seems to have continued its downhill path until it closed less than 40 years later. In 1478 it was described as 'deserted by monks'. It was handed over to the Bishop of Salisbury, and most of its land passed into the ownership of St George's Chapel at Windsor, property of the King. As a consequence, St George's Chapel continued to own much land in and around Newbury for centuries afterwards.

Very little of the medieval Sandleford Priory is now visible. The main building on the site now is an 18th-century house, currently used by St Gabriel's School. Some thick walls in this building indicate that these may have formed part of the priory, but later alterations have removed any other hint of a medieval origin. The 18th-century dining room at the rear was converted from the priory's chapel, and the chapel roof survives hidden but still intact.

★★

Like other villages and towns in the Middle Ages, Newbury was responsible for maintaining law and order, with Wallingford Castle as a centre for administering justice. In the 13th century Nicholas the clerk ('clericus') and Edith, both from Sandleford, were murdered along Newtown Road in Newbury. A contemporary account reveals that 'the evildoers who killed Nicholas and Edith were captured by the men of Newbury and brought to Wallingford and there they were hanged before the justices …'.

Newbury was often described as a borough, even centuries before the first known Charter. There are references to Burgesses in 1189 and to Town Bailiffs in 1204, for example. In 1302, along with many other English boroughs, Newbury sent two MPs to Parliament. This was during the reign of Edward I. In 1337 it sent three representatives to Westminster; however, that was the last time it was represented separately from the county of Berkshire until the 19th century. In 1377, with a population estimated at 1,900, Newbury was larger than Reading and was ranked as the 37th largest town in the country.

There is no comprehensive survey of the effect of the Black Death on Newbury, but the town was badly affected, and the market closed. When William de Hastings, who was Lord of the Manor of Benham Valence (just to the west of Newbury), died in April 1349, a hearing was held concerning his property. It established that he had free tenants in Newbury, who used to pay quarterly rents worth 40 shillings. But these tenants were now all dead, and the property had been seized by the Crown. In addition William had a right to part of the market toll and part of the income from a tan-mill, together worth 26s 6d per year. However, they now raised no income, because of the plague. Like most of the country, the whole of the Newbury area suffered, the severity varying a little from village to village. At nearby Crookham, so many died that much of the land went out of cultivation.

Donnington Castle

In 1386, Sir Richard Abberbury (also written as Adderbury) was granted the right to turn his manor house at Donnington into a castle. The grant was made by King Richard II:

> Know that by our special grace we have granted and given licence ... to our beloved and faithful Richard Abberbury the elder, that he may build anew and fortify with stone and lime and crenellate a certain castle on his own land at Donnington, Berks ... *Henley, June 11, 1386*

Sir Richard's family had become lords of the manor of Donnington about a century earlier, and Sir Richard had inherited the estate by 1353. He was a knight in the service of Edward, the Black Prince, who was almost an exact contemporary. He campaigned with the Black Prince in France in 1359 and 1366, and in recognition the Prince granted him £40 a year for life. The following year, when the Prince gathered an army at Northampton, Abberbury's own contingent consisted of four squires and ten archers. In 1369 Abberbury served again in France, playing a prominent role in a campaign which started badly but went on to capture Limoges.

When the Black Prince died in June 1376, Abberbury remained close to his widow and his young heir, Richard. Abberbury even sold some of his own land to raise money for them. He became one of the three guardians of the future Richard II and was part of the Royal Household after the ten-year-old Richard was crowned King in 1377. In 1380 he was sent abroad to negotiate Richard II's marriage and, as a consequence, he became chamberlain to Richard's first wife, Anne of Bohemia, who Richard married in 1382.

Abberbury's financial position was secured by the grant of property at Iffley and Carswell, confirmed in 1385, and this may be sufficient to justify the start of work on Donnington Castle. However, these were unsettled times. The Peasants' Revolt had taken place in 1381, when the lives of the King and his family were seriously threatened and some advisors killed. There was continuing unrest over high taxation and court extravagance. In 1386 the King's position was once more insecure, building up to a revolt among his nobles. Also in 1386, rumours of an invasion from France were rife. Towns were ordered to repair their walls and arrangements were made for calling out soldiers. It was in these

The 14th-century Donnington Castle, from a Godfrey engraving of 1772.

circumstances that Richard Abberbury was given permission by Richard II to turn his house at Donnington into a castle.

Abberbury built Donnington Castle at a time inspired by the legend of King Arthur, which even then had a knightly appeal. He created an oblong building with an irregular west end, a round tower at each corner, and a rectangular one in the middle of each of the longer sides. The base of the defensive wall can still be seen. Inside this was a courtyard, with stables and living quarters. From the gatehouse wall still facing inside the castle, it is clear that it was a three-storey building, and that at least some of the major rooms were at the gatehouse end – three remaining fireplaces testify to this. The gatehouse, which still stands, was then added to the main building: visitors can see the join at the window on the Newbury side of the castle, where the gatehouse joins and lops off part of the stone 'hood'. The external walls of both parts of the castle are made from the same material – flint – and are built in the same style. Soon after, Abberbury fell from power; in 1388 he was expelled from court by discontented nobles, but returned to a position of influence before his death in 1399.

He died the year before Geoffrey Chaucer, who has a long-established legendary connection with Donnington Castle, even to the extent of stories that Chaucer wrote *The Canterbury Tales* under an oak tree there. This can be dismissed as fanciful romance, but there are genuine Chaucer connections. Firstly, Donnington Castle was later owned by Geoffrey Chaucer's son, Thomas. In addition, Geoffrey Chaucer went abroad on a diplomatic mission with Richard Abberbury or his son of the same name. At Court both Geoffrey Chaucer and the elder Richard Abberbury found themselves opposed by the same group of nobles: so while Geoffrey Chaucer did not own Donnington Castle, there is the real possibility that he was a visitor to Abberbury's Berkshire home.

The younger Sir Richard Abberbury attached himself to John of Gaunt, Duke of Lancaster, and followed him on campaign in 1370. He was granted an income from the Duchy of Lancaster, became a knight of John of Gaunt's chamber and was left a legacy in Gaunt's will. It was Richard Abberbury the son who sold Donnington in 1415 to Thomas Chaucer, and he died the following year.

Chaucer appears to have bought Donnington for his daughter Alice, about the time of her first marriage. She was eleven, and her husband died soon afterwards. Her second marriage was to the Earl of Salisbury, who was killed at the siege of Orleans in France. Her third husband, at the age of 26, was William de la Pole, Earl of Suffolk. Donnington Castle belonged to the de la Poles for the rest of the medieval period, but many of its owners spent more time at homes elsewhere. Surprisingly little is known about daily life at the castle, which as well as providing a fortification, was the manor house for Donnington.

★★

Agriculture was of vital importance for the whole of the area, within the boundaries of modern Newbury as well as around it. Many of the town's medieval fields survived in some form for centuries. There were the arable fields Westfield and Eastfield, pasture at Northcroft and on The Marsh, and a 'waste' at The Wash.

The Westfield was a large area to the west of Bartholomew Street, much of it now occupied by the 'Westfields' housing developments which include Craven Road. This was farmed in strips, and by the end of the Middle Ages had been divided in unequal ways among many different owners. The Eastfield lay between Bartholomew Street and Cheap Street, stretching across the area of the modern St Johns Road. About four acres of this was Nepylls Mead. Eastfield did not extend across to the Boundary Road area, which at that time was in Greenham.

Northcroft, currently the site of the leisure centre, kept its common grazing rights until the 1950s. The Marsh is now known as Victoria Park, but Marsh Lane still survives as a reminder of the old name. It appears to have been common pasture from an early date. Walter Money reported a tradition that the Marsh was given to the town by 'two maiden ladies', but added, 'if so it must have been at a very early period.'

The Wash is now Wash Common, extensively covered by housing. 'The Wash' was originally the southern slope leading down to the River Enborne, which gained its name in the Anglo-Saxon period from the regular flooding there. The nearby common, by extension, became Wash Common but was regularly known as The Wash. The soil was poor, leaving it as unwanted for agriculture, and it survived as common 'waste' into the 19th century.

The making of cloth was practised locally from prehistoric times, along with the raising of sheep. For most of the Middle Ages the cloth made in the Newbury area was of local rather than national importance, although Berkshire sheep contributed to the country's export of wool, upon which the economy depended.

The spread of fulling mills in England from the late 12th century onwards, was associated with the rising importance of the cloth industry in the later Middle Ages. These mills used wooden hammers to pound the surface of the cloth and give it a more professional finish. Three mills together at West Mills in Newbury all became fulling mills, while the Town Mills continued as corn mills. The embankment at West Mills which now serves as the south bank of the canal, appears to have been created in the Middle Ages to raise the head of water for the mills. At Greenham two mills became fulling mills while two remained corn mills. Many of the other mills in the area were also converted to fulling. Dyehouses were set up for specialist dyers who used blue woad as their main dye. In the 15th century, several cloth-producers, or clothiers, became relatively wealthy men by local standards.

Spinning was an occupation which was probably carried out mainly as outwork, but artisan weavers had their own small workshops and there were also clothworking workshops, often close to the fulling mills, which used teasels to raise the nap of the cloth and then the oversized fullers' shears to crop it to add quality to the finish. A woollen cloth called kersey was among the cloths produced in Newbury.

There was a range of other industries in the town. The town centre had a long history of metalworking in the Middle Ages, which included iron smelting, as well as forging. At the north end of Bartholomew Street, copper alloy was being cast and worked.

Tanning mills in Newbury are mentioned from at least the 13th century onwards. In 1297 they appear among the Newbury property owned by

In the Tudor period there were three fulling mills processing cloth at West Mills; a later corn mill can still be seen in this mid-20th-century view across the River Kennet.

the wealthy William Mortimer at the time of his death. Mortimer had been receiving 13 shillings from the toll of Newbury market and 10 shillings from the tanning mills among other income from the town. There are several references to the same mills in the 14th century, and the processing of leather continued as an important industry for the town.

In the Middle Ages the local London Clay was used at several locations near Newbury to make pottery, as it had been for centuries before. Excavations on the route of the Newbury bypass in the 1990s revealed evidence of an industry producing coarse pottery for local use. 'Dumps' of rejected bowls and jars were found north and south of Reddings Copse at Enborne, near Wheatlands Lane and Enborne Street. These were filled with unglazed utilitarian kitchen wares which have been described as aiming at the lower and middle class markets. Bowl-shaped pits containing charcoal and showing signs of burning were identified as possible kilns. Clay tiles were also found.

The first Newbury Bridge was built during the Middle Ages and although the date is not known, there is a reference to it being repaired in the 14th century. It was a wooden bridge, and like others of its kind it would have been regularly weather-damaged, repaired and even replaced, with (for Newbury) new timber taken from Wash Common. By the end of the Middle Ages, as in many places elsewhere, there were properties along the bridge.

Wars of the Roses

Newbury had mixed fortunes during the 15th-century struggles known as the Wars of the Roses. The year 1460 was a time of particular uncertainty and conflict, and the town suffered for supporting Richard, Duke of York, who at that time was also Newbury's Lord of the Manor. With King Henry VI's backing, the Earl of Wiltshire came to Newbury to seek out traitors: those who had shown friendship or support for the Duke of York, or his followers. Of those found guilty, some were hanged, drawn and quartered, and many others found their possessions confiscated. This has been described by some as 'judicial terrorism', while others refer to it as the 'harrying' of Newbury. The manor of Newbury was seized by the King.

Richard of York died later the same year, but when his son became king as Edward IV the following year, Newbury came back into the family's ownership: Edward IV gave it to his mother Cecily, Duchess of York.

Just over 20 years later Newbury was supporting a rebellion against another Richard of York, King Richard III. The Duke of Buckingham led the rising, raising his standard at Brecon in Wales, and Newbury was one of the other main meeting places for the rebels on 18 October 1483, along with Exeter, Salisbury and sites in Surrey and Kent. The aim was to place Henry Tudor (later King Henry VII) on the throne, but the plot failed and Buckingham was captured and beheaded at Salisbury. A cluster of the gentry from the Thames Valley met at Newbury to support Henry's claim. Among them was Sir William Norris (also Norreys) of Yattendon, whose family provided part of the name of Hampstead Norreys. He was at court under Edward IV, and was twice Sheriff of Berkshire. For his part in the Duke of Buckingham's rebellion he was declared a traitor, had his estates confiscated and fled abroad. When he came back with Henry Tudor in 1485, his estates were returned and his fortunes rose again. He was one of the commanders of Henry VII's army at the battle of Stoke Field in 1487, which finally put an end to the Yorkist claim. Others who joined the abortive rebellion at Newbury in 1483 included Thomas de la Mare (also Delamare) of Aldermaston, and Lord St Amand, whose family property included West Woodhay. John Harcourt of Stanton Harcourt in Oxfordshire was another, who was outlawed for his actions at Newbury, and whose son Robert was standard bearer to Henry Tudor at the battle of Bosworth in 1485. The Newbury rebels included others from Oxfordshire and Wiltshire, and even the serving mayor of Southampton.

Chapter 3

Newbury in the Tudor period: Religion and Cloth

The Tudor period locally saw many voices calling for religious change, but those in power frequently responded with persecution. In 1491 a dozen people from the Newbury area were charged with heresy. Newbury man Thomas Tailor was tried for saying that it was better to give to the poor than go on pilgrimage, that men were deceived by priests, and that the priesthood was not ordained by God. Tailor was a fuller, working on the production of woollen cloth. He was ordered to go bare-footed, bare-legged and bare-headed, with a bundle of faggots on his back and a stick in his hand, into the parish church of Newbury and Newbury's market place, and publicly renounce his views. He was to do the same in Reading Abbey and market place, Wokingham market place, and Ramsbury and Sonning churches. When he had finished, he was ordered to say five Pater Nosters, five Ave Marias and one Credo every day for the rest of his life.

The day of Tailor's trial the Bishop of Salisbury sent an order to Newbury, Speen, Shaw and Thatcham to look for more 'heretics and traitors'. Within days, six more men from the Newbury area appeared before the Bishop. They were Augustine Stere and Henry Benet of Speen, William Brigger of Thatcham, and Richard Hignell, William Prior and Richard Goddard of Newbury. Most had been critical of priests and images, and said that the consecrated bread for the Mass could not contain the real body of Christ. All six were given sentences similar to Tailor. Three more men from Newbury were accused of heresies in February. They were ordered to do bare-footed penances through several towns in the area, including Newbury's market place and St Nicolas' church.

Later in February came the cases of Alice Hignell and William Carpenter, both of Newbury. Alice Hignell had criticised those lighting candles to an image of St Leonard as fools, saying, 'When St Leonard will eat a candle and blow out another, then I will offer him a candle…' She was ordered to do penance, including a bread-and-water fast on the vigil of St Leonard.

Punishments for heresy did not ease after King Henry VIII took the throne in 1509. Christopher Shoemaker, who is said to have lived at Great Missenden in Buckinghamshire before moving to Newbury, was charged with having read out words which Christ spoke to his disciples. In addition, he is said to have argued against transubstantiation, pilgrimages, and the worship of images. For these things he was condemned to death, and he was burned at the stake at Newbury in 1518.

One of the almsmen from Donnington Hospital was accused in 1538 of spreading a rumour that King Henry VIII was dead. Thomas Barrie was sentenced to stand all day in Newbury Market Place with his ears nailed to the pillory. At the end of the day he was released by having both his ears cut off.

Poughley Priory was a small monastery in the part of Chaddleworth now within the perimeter of RAF Welford. Poughley, which like Sandleford was a priory for Augustinian canons, owned substantial property along the Lambourn valley and throughout the area. It was suppressed early in Henry VIII's reign, in 1524, when Henry's chief minister Thomas Wolsey acquired its lands. Shortly afterwards Wolsey was impeached and charged with high treason, and his property (including Poughley) was forfeited to the Crown. King Henry VIII wanted land in Westminster, belonging to Westminster Abbey, for his own use. So in 1531 he exchanged the Poughley estates with Westminster Abbey in a deal which gave him what he wanted, and made the Abbey the owner of a substantial amount of Berkshire land. This included property at Bagnor, Boxford, Brightwalton, Chaddleworth, Chieveley, Colthrop, Curridge, Eastbury, East Garston, Hampstead Norreys, Hamstead Marshall, Lambourn, Leckhampstead, Maidencourt (near Great Shefford), Midgham, Oare, Peasemore and Poughley. At Bagnor, Westminster Abbey gained two fulling mills, one of which (in a rebuilt version) is now the Watermill Theatre.

Far more grand, powerful and wealthy was Reading Abbey, which owned a considerable amount of central Berkshire. When the Abbot was executed in November 1539 and its land subsequently offered for sale, this included the manors of Reading, Beenham, Bucklebury, Burghfield, Cholsey, Pangbourne, Sulhamstead, Tilehurst, Thatcham and Ufton Nervet, as well as other land in Berkshire and as far afield as Norfolk and Leicestershire.

Rebuilding St Nicolas' church

Newbury's parish church of St Nicolas was completely rebuilt in the Tudor period, in the Perpendicular style. It consists of a chancel with north and south chapels, an aisled nave of five bays with north and south porches, and a western tower. Symbols of Queen Catherine of Aragon indicate that work started after 1509, during the reign of Henry VIII. Newbury clothier John Winchcombe I (also known as Smallwood) left £40 in his will 'towards the building and edifying' of St Nicolas' church. It was a substantial sum, but would have paid for only a small fraction of the work. Other wills show contributions from John May (40 shillings); John Sparrow (2 shillings); Isabel Hunt ('my best pans'); William Miller of Shaw (6s 8d); Alice Stillman (12 pence) Robert Coke (6s 8d); William Dolman (40 shillings); John Seman (7 shillings); John Stowre (13s 4d); and John Benett (20 shillings). This sequence of wills, while not a complete list of contributions, suggests a construction period running from 1520 until 1534. Inside the church, on the east wall of the tower overlooking the nave, is a stone which carries the date 1532, providing separate corroboration for this timescale.

In the roof of the nave of St Nicolas' church are painted wooden bosses, which carry two devices. One of these is an 'S' overlaying a capital

St Nicolas' church, before Victorian alterations.

'I', giving an 'IS' for John Smallwood (John Winchcombe I). The other has a Greek sigma over a capital 'I' (so depicting 'IS' in another form), which is a device used as the merchant's mark for John Winchcombe II (c.1489–1557). Arranging these devices in an alternating pattern suggests that the main patron was John Winchcombe II, sponsoring the work to his own glory and that of his father John Winchcombe I (d.1520).

Writing in the 1660s, historian Thomas Fuller wrote that Jack of Newbury '…built the Church of Newberry from the Pulpit Westward to the Tower inclusively …'.

★★

Jack of Newbury

'Jack of Newbury' was a wealthy businessman and exporter who mixed with some of the most important people in Tudor England. The middle of the 16th century was a period when the production of woollen cloth dominated England's economy, and her overseas trade. John Winchcombe II, otherwise known as Jack of Newbury, was the leading figure nationally in this overwhelmingly important trade. He deserves a prominent place in the economic history of the country.

He was a clothier, coordinating the different stages in the production of cloths, and personally identified with the final product, which were known abroad as 'Winchcombes'. The high international reputation of these cloths appears plainly at Antwerp in 1538, when English merchants agreed that they would only sell Winchcombes to those who would take an equal number of inferior cloths. Two years later traders had to buy two inferior cloths in order to purchase each Winchcombe. Customers included some of the most prominent national figures. Among John Winchcombe's orders in 1539 was one for 1,000 cloths from Henry VIII's chief minister, Thomas Cromwell.

John Winchcombe was producing woollen cloths called kersies, each cloth about a yard wide and 17–18 yards long. In the middle of the 16th century, 200 years before the beginning of the Industrial Revolution, surviving statistics show that John Winchcombe was producing at least 6,000 Winchcombe kersies a year, or an average of 500 cloths a month. This was at a time normally associated with cottage industry, or 'domestic' industry. Most of the kersies were sent to London, where they were exported to Antwerp, and from there they were sent into Germany and eastern Europe, or south to the Mediterranean states, even as far as the Middle East.

As a clothier, John Winchcombe used a combination of outworkers (for example, for spinning), regular contractors (fulling), and his own workers (combers). There are legends of a massive weaving workshop, featuring 200 looms, which may be an exaggeration but probably have a basis in truth. In addition, Winchcombe was closely involved in the process of dyeing. He leased his own dyehouse, and his kersies were most commonly dyed in shades of blue, with woad as the main dye. The scale of his production is emphasized by one order for dye in 1549, which was for 541 cwt of woad: over 27 tons. He also had cartloads of dye delivered regularly from the port at Southampton. Clothmaking had been an occupation in Newbury for centuries, but it is through Winchcombe (and the quantity and overseas reputation of his cloths) that the Newbury industry gained short-lived national importance.

The industry was heavily regulated in the 16th century. As a prominent clothier, John Winchcombe successfully organised and led a national petition to overturn a new law for clothmakers imposed in the mid-1530s. He gained signatures from kersey-producers across six counties, mainly in central southern England, and put their case to the Privy Council. The Council records show that 'Winchcombe of Newbury and sundry other clothiers did make suit unto the King's highness ...' The individual names for the clothiers from four of the six counties survive, a total of 80. The Privy Council records the names of the other two counties which were involved, and all were led by Winchcombe.

His wealth led him to acquire land, available for purchase following the Dissolution of the Monasteries. In 1540 he bought Bucklebury and Thatcham, which until then belonged to Reading Abbey. The purchase went through for £2,619 13s 4d, less than three months after the execution of the Abbot. Much of the estates at Bucklebury have been owned by the Winchcombe family and its relations ever since. He bought Farnborough for about £400; and he bought Lockinge and Ginge for over £1,000. He had plenty of additional property besides, some of it leased from St George's Chapel at Windsor. In Newbury he leased property in Northbrook Street, Bartholomew Street and Cheap Street, with land in the East and West Fields. He had more property in Greenham, Enborne and Kintbury.

His home was a large building on the east side of Northbrook Street (a site now partly occupied by Marks & Spencer). This was a high status building, arranged around courtyards, between Marsh Lane and Jack Street. The main hall was decorated with carved wood panelling and tapestries. Some of the carvings are now at Sudeley Castle in Gloucestershire. A small part of this large building still survives, at

Jack of Newbury's house (now 24 Northbrook Street), as it looked in the early 20th century.

the corner of Marsh Lane (now occupied by Monsoon), with moulded and carved ornamentation which still gives a hint of its 16th-century display.

Winchcombe's business and his wealth led him to mix with powerful people, such as Sir Thomas Gresham, who later founded the Royal Exchange: records show him gambling at dice with Winchcombe (and losing). He loaned money to King Henry VIII. And the future Protector Somerset visited Winchcombe at home in Northbrook Street, handing out money to some of Winchcombe's workers. As his business prospered, Winchcombe did not put it aside; he combined his business position with the status of one of the county gentry. He was invited with other Berkshire gentry to the reception for Henry VIII's fourth wife, Anne of Cleves. He acquired a coat of arms, became a Justice of the Peace and a Member of Parliament. And, as one of the gentry, he was invited to supply soldiers for various royal armies: to oppose the 'northern rebels' (Pilgrimage of Grace) in 1536, to fight in Flanders in 1543 and to fight in France in 1544.

It is a distorted version of this last which supplied the basis for the old legend of Jack of Newbury leading Newbury men to the Battle of Flodden. On both occasions, England was at war with France and Scotland. On both occasions, one of the leading figures involved was Charles Brandon, Duke of Suffolk. In 1544 Brandon was leading English forces for the capture of the French port of Boulogne, and John Winchcombe provided part of the army. Some of the surviving documents name 100 and some 150 of the men he took, first to Dover and then across the Channel. They include people working in various parts of the cloth industry in Newbury. These served as gunners, archers, pikemen and men armed with clubs, headed by a standard-bearer, fife and drums. As captain, Winchcombe appears to have been on horseback and armed as a demi-lance. And he provided his men with new coats for the occasion. It is this expedition which provided the basis for one part of Winchcombe's coat of arms: a *fleurs-de-lis* between two spearheads.

Jack of Newbury became a legendary character at the hands of Thomas Deloney, an entertainer who in the 1590s published 'The Pleasant History of John Winchcombe, in his younger years called Jack of Newbery, The famous and worthy Clothier of England ...'. Jack of Newbury was described by a 17th-century historian as 'the most considerable clothier England ever beheld'. As the legend grew, the story was distorted. He became a celebrated character along the lines of Robin Hood or Dick Whittington. Pubs were named after him, along with an opera, a racehorse, a locomotive and even a vegetable (a swede). At the same time,

A portrait of John Winchcombe (Jack of Newbury) in 1550, aged 61. (By kind permission of Mr and Mrs Willie Hartley Russell)

he was accepted by many historians as having founded England's first factory.

The story of Jack became entangled with John Winchcombe's father of the same name (John Winchcombe I, or John Smallwood), a clothier who died in 1520. This John Winchcombe was a prosperous figure locally, but had none of the national standing or the wealth of his son. When modern historians came to look for evidence to support the legend they found none, because they were looking in the period before 1520. In recent years the Jack of Newbury story has consequently been interpreted largely as fiction, rather than based on history.

The confusion between the two John Winchcombes continues. There is an original portrait of John Winchcombe II, painted in 1550 when he was 61. This was traditionally and correctly identified as a portrait of Jack of Newbury, and it formed the basis for the signs of pubs and inns of that name. When his father (John Winchcombe I) became wrongly identified as Jack of Newbury, this was described as a portrait of Jack of Newbury's son. Now, once again, it can be identified as a portrait of Jack of Newbury himself (John Winchcombe II). The father is represented by a memorial brass now under the tower in St Nicolas' church.

The Newbury Martyrs

The reign of Queen Mary, Henry VIII's daughter, has a long-remembered association with religious persecutions. Julius Palmer, Thomas Robyns (normally referred to as Thomas Askew) and John Gwyn were three Protestants who were tried in Newbury in 1556 for their religious views, convicted, and executed by being burned at the stake. Their trial took place in St Nicolas' church, where the panel of judges was headed by Dr William Jeffrey, who represented the Bishop of Salisbury. With him were John Winchcombe II and his son John Winchcombe III, Sir Richard Brydges, Sir William Rainsford and the parson of Englefield, the Rev. Clement Burdett.

Palmer had been briefly Master of Reading School, and it is in relation to him that most detail survives. On 16 July 1556, he was brought before the judges; a transcript of the hearing, taken down at the time, still exists. It was Dr Jeffrey who opened the proceedings and put the charges: 'First, that you deny the Pope's holiness supremacy; Next, that there are but two sacraments; Thirdly, that the priest sheweth up an idol at mass, and therefore you went to no mass since your first coming to Reading; Fourthly, that there is no purgatory; Last of all, that you be a sower of sedition, and have sought to divide the unity of the queen's subjects.'

In his defence Palmer wanted to argue his religious views, but he was restricted by the judges' refusal to allow for theological debate. Dr Jeffrey contended that Palmer was charged with defying the Church. Proving the authenticity of his beliefs, even if he could do so, would not lead to him being declared innocent.

Palmer was called on to put his name to a list of 'heresies' for which he was condemned. He refused, saying that the beliefs listed were not his own, and he could not sign. Dr Jeffrey is recorded as saying, 'Ye may see, good people, what shifts these heretics seek to escape burning, when they see justice ministered unto them.' Palmer remained adamant in his beliefs, and his opposition to the Pope. Finally Palmer signed his name, but wrote underneath a list of his own beliefs and his objections to some of the points against him.

The same day, the three men walked to their place of execution, and a crowd gathered around them. They reached the Sandpits, in Enborne Road, beyond where the Lamb public house, stands now. There the three prisoners

In 1984, a community play was performed by Newbury Community Theatre re-enacting the story of the Newbury martyrs. This still from the play shows the men being taken for trial at St Nicolas' church. (Geoff Fletcher, via David Wylie)

were chained to a pole. Faggots were thrown around them, and the fire was lit. According to a later account, as the fire began to take hold, all three lifted their hands towards heaven, and began to pray: 'Lord Jesu strengthen us, Lord Jesu assist us, Lord Jesu receive our souls.' They continued praying, without struggling, until they died. A small plaque to them survives near the junction of Enborne Road and Rockingham Road.

★★

Thomas Dolman was a Newbury clothier who made his money in the Tudor cloth industry, with much of the cloth produced for export. Like Winchcombe, Dolman was producing woollen cloth on an industrial scale. The account book of Thomas Gresham, a merchant adventurer, shows over 4,000 cloths ordered from Dolman from 1547 to 1550. This can be combined with other statistics to show that Dolman was producing over 2,500 kersey cloths per year.

As a clothier, Dolman was the entrepreneur who co-ordinated all the people involved in the different stages of cloth production: wool combing, spinning, weaving, fulling, dyeing and finishing. Some of the earlier parts of this process were probably carried out in the workers' own homes, but the cloth was processed in fulling mills along the River Kennet. Thomas Dolman leased two fulling mills for his cloths at Greenham Mills (a site now occupied by flats), where he also leased two corn mills. In addition, in 1557 he was granted a fulling mill at Colthrop.

His cloths were dyed before export, and his dyehouse was in Cheap Street, Newbury, where the dyer at the time of his death in 1575 was William Rigsby. The scale of Dolman's clothmaking is confirmed by one order in 1549 for nearly nine tons of his main dye, woad. Additional records show woad being delivered by the cartload from Southampton. Woad produced various shades of blue, his main colour. Six woad vats, two other vats, a furnace of copper and another of brass along with other implements in the dyehouse are all mentioned in Dolman's will.

He was one of the five Newbury clothiers listed in the petition organised by his colleague John Winchcombe II, to change the law regulating the cloth industry. Dolman dealt with customers like Thomas Gresham, who exported the kersies from London to Antwerp. The 1540s was a boom time for cloth production, and the Antwerp market simply could not get enough of kersies made in Newbury. Clothiers like Dolman became very rich. Some of the money went in the 1550s towards the purchase of the manors of Shaw and Colthrop (1554), together with additional land in both manors in 1557, which included the purchase of Shaw Mills (at that time 'two corn mills under one roof'). In 1558 Dolman bought Frethorne manor in Childrey and the manors of Stanton and Snowshill in Gloucestershire, and in 1568 Speen ('Churchspeen') was sold to him and his second son jointly.

Dolman also leased property in Northbrook Street in Newbury. A deed of 1543 refers to a building in Northbrook Street lately occupied by Thomas Dolman or his assigns. Another building on the east side of Northbrook Street is referred to in a survey of c.1550. Thomas Dolman I can also be linked to St Nicolas' church, where he was churchwarden in 1552. His will was written in January 1571, but he lived for several more years. A memorandum added in November 1575 described him as sick in body, and he died shortly afterwards, with the will proved on 23 December.

Thomas Dolman I left the manor or estate of Shaw to his son of the same name, born in 1543. It was this Thomas Dolman who built Shaw House (completed in 1581) with the wealth from the cloth trade which he inherited on his father's death. The fine brick mansion just north of Newbury is the largest Elizabethan house in Berkshire, and still retains

Shaw House in the early 19th century (above) and as it looks today (below).

much of its Elizabethan character, especially when seen from the south. The recent restoration has confirmed its date and supplied much more information about the house and the way it has changed over the years. Thomas Dolman II's first wife Margaret was the daughter of William Forster of Aldermaston, from an established local family, and Thomas became one of the Berkshire county gentry, granted a coat of arms in 1587 and appointed Sheriff of Berkshire in 1588, the year of the Spanish Armada. He died in 1622.

The middle of the 16th century saw a major interruption in the cloth industry, caused by a combination of factors which included the disruption of the international market in Antwerp, and changes in currency exchange rates. This meant an economic recession from 1551. The result was large-scale unemployment locally, and in the years that followed a letter was sent by the Privy Council to some of the local gentry urging action: '... if you shall find that they which were accustomed to keep men occupying in draping and other works thereto belonging do give over the trade thereof, and so occasion any number of persons to live idly whereof disorder may arise, then we would that you should ... send for the principal clothiers that so do give over their trade and use all the good reasons that you can to induce them to recontinue their trade and not thus suddenly in this time of the year, to use such hard dealings with their neighbours ...'. The letter came shortly after the death of John Winchcombe II in 1557. John's son Henry attempted to continue the business, but he also died (in 1562). Newbury's cloth industry quickly lost its national standing, although it continued to have local importance.

Donnington has its own link to the defeat of the Spanish Armada in 1588. In 1600 the manor of Donnington, including the castle, was given by Queen Elizabeth to Charles Howard, Baron Howard of Effingham and later Earl of Nottingham. He was the commander-in-chief of the English fleet, and the gesture was intended as a reward for his services, particularly in defeating the Armada. It was under Lord Howard that Donnington Hospital was re-founded.

For centuries, the centre of Newbury's Market Place was occupied by a building now normally referred to as the Guildhall, which served as a town hall in its time. It may have been first constructed in the 15th century, funded by a bequest in 1485. As its name suggests, the building was associated with a local guild or combination of guilds. Among Newbury's guilds was a Guild of St George, open to members of any craft. As the weathervane on the Guildhall was in the form of a dragon, it is tempting to link the two.

The Guildhall was rebuilt in 1611 (during the reign of James I), taking the form which appears in a number of paintings and drawings. If it was rebuilt by Newbury Corporation, the timing is appropriate. Newbury had been granted its first Charter by Queen Elizabeth in 1596, and the Mayor and Corporation were still in the process of gaining control of the town. The main part of the building consisted of a Council Chamber on the first floor, which was used by the Corporation and for courts. This chamber was supported on pillars forming an open 'shambles' at ground level, used for markets; meat, poultry and butter were among items for sale. The first floor chamber had three tile-hung gables along the western side.

Outside the Council Chamber on the west side was a balcony, with a pillory (to secure an offender's head and hands) at its southern end. On the ground, at the northern end opposite the site now occupied by NatWest Bank, were the stocks (to pin their legs). In addition the Guildhall was the site for the whipping post. The building was eventually demolished in 1828.

Queen Elizabeth granted the earliest charter to the Borough of Newbury in 1596. It outlined government of the town by a council consisting of 31 burgesses, which included the mayor and six aldermen. There were to be five companies for the principal trades: 1. tanners (including barbers and surgeons); 2. mercers (including all provision dealers and apothecaries); 3. tailors (including scriveners and schoolmasters); 4. weavers and clothmakers; 5. braziers (including builders).

The Charter confirmed four fairs, with the proceeds going to the Corporation or Borough. The first Mayor of Newbury, heading the new Corporation, was Bartholomew Yate.

The former Tudor Cafe in Northbrook Street (now occupied by Clarks and Accessorize) is probably originally Elizabethan, although it has never been properly assessed. The Eight Bells in Bartholomew Street, which was a pub for centuries before closing in 1961, is a building originally from the late 16th or early 17th century, altered and then restored. And Bartholomew Manor in Argyle Road, which has endured many changes over the centuries, is genuinely Tudor inside.

Chapter 4

The Civil War Century

In the early 17th century the cloth industry in Newbury was in decline, and clothier John Kendrick decided to help those who were suffering as a consequence. He left money in his will to Newbury and Reading to provide buildings where unemployed workers from the industry could find work. In Reading this 'work-house' was called The Oracle. In Newbury, Kendrick left £4,000 to create 'a commodious house and garden to set poor people on work'. A site near the Market Place was purchased and in 1626-7 a large timber-framed building was erected with three wings, with master carpenter Richard Emmes of Speenhamland in charge. It provided facilities for making and finishing cloth, starting with the raw wool, but soon ran into problems. This was the origin of the building known as the Cloth Hall, now part of the museum, which is the only surviving one of the three wings.

Unemployment and poverty came to a head in Newbury in 1630, when hungry locals stopped and looted the corn carts going from Newbury to Reading. The ring-leaders were mostly from Speen and Greenham, and a number of elderly women from Newbury were among those punished.

Newbury USA

A group which founded Newbury in Massachusetts, USA, set sail in 1634. It was led by Rev. Thomas Parker, and Rev. James and Nicholas Noyes. Thomas Parker, born in 1595, was Master of the Grammar School (based at the Litten). He was also curate to Dr William Twisse (1578?-1646), the Rector of Newbury, who preached at St Nicolas' church. Twisse was a nationally-prominent and controversial Puritan clergyman.

With Rev. James Noyes and Noyes' brother Nicholas and others from Berkshire, Wiltshire and Gloucestershire, Parker set sail in 1634 on the *Mary and John*. They landed first at the site of the modern Ipswich in Massachusetts, where they were joined by other prospective settlers. In 1635 they moved on to a nearby place then called Quascacunquen. A traditional story states that the settlers arrived through Plum Island Sound in open boats and landed on the north bank of what is now the Parker River in May or June 1635. Here they founded the new Newbury on the banks of a river which was named after Thomas Parker.

Parker's nephew John Woodbridge was among those who took land in Newbury, and he became the new town's first town clerk. Woodbridge came back to England on the death of his father but by 1642 he had returned to New England. With his younger brother Benjamin, John would recross the Atlantic to England in 1647, once the success of Parliament in the Civil War had made the country more acceptable to the Puritans in religious terms. For several years John followed in his uncle's footsteps in this country as Master of Newbury Grammar School, while Benjamin Woodbridge succeeded Dr Twisse to become Rector of Newbury. The American town, named Newbury in honour of Parker, who died in 1677, was later outgrown by its own suburb, Newburyport, a few miles to the north.

★★

In the 1640s the Civil War between the King and Parliament began. Newbury was the location for two major battles of these wars, with thousands taking part on each side. In both cases, there was no clear winner, which helps to explain why these are not as well known nationally as battles such as Naseby or Marston Moor.

The First Battle of Newbury, 1643

In September 1643 King Charles I and a Royalist army were laying siege to Gloucester. In London, Parliament brought together an army to relieve the city, and command was given to the Earl of Essex. Included were some of the London Trained Bands, a well-established and trained militia, together with some hastily-raised auxiliaries, many of them London apprentices. This army marched across England, and the Royalist army lifted the siege as they arrived. Gloucester was rescued. But London had been left poorly defended.

The Parliamentary army started back for London, crossing the country again. The Royalists decided to stop them before they reached the capital, and force a confrontation. Prince Rupert, nephew of Charles I, led his cavalry in an attack on the moving column in Aldbourne Chase, delaying their progress. Essex, held up by the attack, crossed the Kennet at Hungerford and kept the river on his left flank as his army marched towards Newbury. By way of Kintbury and Hamstead Marshall they came to Enborne, and sent ahead to Newbury to get provisions ready for men and horses.

The Royalist army headed for Newbury by way of Wantage, and Prince Rupert's cavalry went ahead to seize Newbury before Essex's army could arrive. That night, the Parliamentary army's camp stretched from Hamstead Park across Enborne to Biggs Hill, with most soldiers out in the open. The Royalists were mainly to the south and west of Newbury, and partly in the town. King Charles stayed at the home of the Mayor of Newbury, Gabriel Cox. Lord Falkland was given accommodation in Cheap Street, at the home of Mr Head.

The First Battle of Newbury was fought on 20 September 1643 and lasted throughout the daylight hours. The battlefield was south from the Kennet up to and across Wash Common, mainly between the Andover Road and the route of the modern A34 (Newbury bypass). Parts of it have been developed (for example, in the Elizabeth Avenue area), while large areas are currently still open fields.

It was a major battle of the Civil War, with estimates of the numbers involved varying, but most writers opting for a figure in the region of 28,000. King Charles took personal command of the Royalist army, with Prince Rupert leading his cavalry. On the Parliamentary side, Essex himself commanded the right while Skippon commanded the left.

The battle began with the Parliamentary army's seizure of Round Hill, a key position in the events of the day. Wash Common is a plateau, but it has a spur which juts out on the north-west corner and commands a large area of ground all the way down to the River Kennet. From the position of the Parliamentary forces below, this spur looked like a 'round hill'. It was especially important for artillery, but the Royalists had failed to notice its significance. At daybreak, Parliamentary forces under Skippon advanced and seized it.

The armies engaged, and the Royalists had early successes on both wings, on Wash Common and on the slope towards the Kennet. In the centre, Round Hill was strongly defended and attacks met with heavy casualties.

The narrative of the battle is not straightforward because of the patchy and sometimes contradictory nature of some of the contemporary sources, which only allow a clear understanding of what was happening to some of the regiments some of the time. The key areas of the battle were Skinners Green, Round Hill, Wash Common, and the area immediately north of the common, much of which at this time was divided into small fields, with high hedges dividing them.

First Battle of Newbury 1643: the view facing north-west across ground lined with hedges that saw the most bitter of the fighting. It was here that Lord Falkland died. In the background is Round Hill where, sited to the left of the present house, Parliamentary artillery was able to help fend off the continuous Royalist attacks.

Skippon called the Red and Blue Regiments of the London Trained Bands, which had been held in reserve, up to the centre part of the battlefield. They fought separately at first, but joined together as they came under heavy attack from Royalist infantry and cavalry. They formed one large square, with pikemen holding off Royalist cavalry. At one stage they were forced back, but rallied and advanced again. They suffered badly from Royalist artillery fire, from a battery not far from where the Falkland Memorial stands today, but were helped when Skippon brought up Parliament's heavier artillery to Round Hill.

As darkness fell and the fighting petered out, little had been gained by either side. Essentially, they had fought each other to a stalemate, or a draw. Nothing appeared to have been resolved.

One incident during the battle drew much attention from contemporaries and historians. On the Royalist side, Sir John Byron's troop was serving as part of Prince Rupert's cavalry, and Lord Falkland rode with him. Byron

The First Battle of Newbury, as recreated by the Sealed Knot in September 1993. (© David Peacock)

himself described how the Royalist foot had been driven out of a field, with Parliamentary soldiers lining the hedge. When he went to investigate, his horse was shot in the throat. Then '…my Lord Falkland (more gallantly than advisedly) spurred his horse through the gap, where he and his horse were immediately killed.' Falkland had strong connections to both the Parliamentary and the Royalist sides, and the deep personal impact the Civil War made on him has led to suggestions that he was (at the least) reckless with his own safety.

As night fell King Charles called a Council of War. Some Royalists wanted to keep their positions, ready to continue the struggle the next day. This was opposed by Lord Percy, General of Ordnance. He argued that the artillery was short of powder and ammunition. Eighty barrels of powder had been used, 20 more than at Edgehill the previous year. Lord Percy and his faction won the backing of the King, and during the early hours of darkness the army marched away towards Oxford.

The next morning Essex and the Parliamentary army continued on their way back to London, avoiding Newbury, and keeping the Kennet on their left. They started along Monks Lane (then Monkey Lane), and across Greenham Common towards Brimpton and Aldermaston.

Contemporary accounts refer to 30 cartloads of Royalist dead and maimed taken away the same day. One Parliamentary soldier saw another 20 more carts filled with dead the next day, and witnessed 30 bodies thrown into one pit and 14 buried in a ditch where they fell. Apart from bodies buried in such ditches and pits, others are said to have been cast down a well.

Some of the dead were buried in the churchyard of St Nicolas, according to the churchwardens' accounts, and Essex gave written orders to the churchwardens of Enborne to bury 'all the dead bodies lying in and around Enborne and Newbury Wash'.

There are a number of earth mounds on Wash Common, within the battlefield, which have now been identified as a Bronze Age cemetery. However, Walter Money wrote in 1881: 'In the year 1855 when Wash Common was enclosed, the levelling of these receptacles of the dead was commenced for the purpose of making a road; but the desecration was stayed by the then owner of the land. The workmen, however, found indications of the bodies having been thrown in a heap and the earth cast over them, the floor of the mound being the natural surface. Human bones, soldiers' buttons, buckles, and portions of accoutrements, bullets, and cannon balls were mixed with the soil which was removed.' This accounts for the inscriptions on the stone tablets on the mounds on the Recreation Ground, linking them to the Civil War.

The more prominent casualties are listed by name, but most are not known. On the Royalist side, Falkland's body was found the next day, taken to a farmhouse at the edge of Wash Common (Falkland Garth/ Falkland House), and then, like others, brought down to the Guildhall in the centre of the Market Place where it lay alongside the bodies of Lord Carnarvon and Lord Sunderland. From there it was moved to the Bear inn at Speenhamland, to be sent back via Oxford to Falkland's estate at Great Tew. In addition to Lord Carnarvon and Lord Sunderland, Colonel Thomas Morgan, Lieutenant Colonel Edward Feilding and Henry Bertie were also among the Royalist dead. Parliamentary dead included Lieutenant-Colonels Joseph Bamfield and William Tucker, and Captains George Mosse, Peter Ware and Francis St Barbe. Estimates for the number of dead vary immensely and it is difficult to be precise, but generally historians would accept a total in the region of 2,500.

The Falkland Memorial, at the junction of the Andover Road and Essex Street, was unveiled in September 1878. It consists of a stone needle

The Falkland Memorial in memory of Lord Falkland and others who died in the 1643 Civil War battle is sited at the junction of Andover Road and Essex Street.

mounted on steps, made from about 40 tons of granite. It was designed by Newbury architect James Money, brother of the historian Walter Money, who purchased the ground and was energetic in getting it established. Walter Money wished to commemorate all who fell in the battle, but the Earl of Carnarvon became closely involved, and it is due to him that the memorial actually celebrates the Royalist side alone. The inscription (on the side facing the shops) reads: *'In memory of those who, on the 20th September, 1643, fell fighting in the army of King Charles I on the field of Newbury, and especially of Lucius Cary, Viscount Falkland, who died here in the 34th year of his age, this monument is set up by those to whom the Majesty of the Crown and the liberties of their country are dear.'*

Another inscription (in Latin) translates as: 'A war is righteous when it is necessary, and sacred are the arms of warriors who have no hope left but in arms.'

The Falkland Memorial was unveiled by Lord Carnarvon, and

afterwards there was a celebratory lunch at the Corn Exchange, attended by about 700 people.

The Second Battle of Newbury, 1644

The following year, King Charles and the Royalist army arrived in Newbury on 22 October. They came from Kingsclere, and Charles spread his army across northern Newbury, from Shaw House to the village of Speen, about 10,000 strong.

Sensing an opportunity, Parliament drew different armies together to outnumber the King's forces: the Earl of Manchester from Reading, Sir William Waller from Shaftesbury and the Earl of Essex from Portsmouth: although Essex himself would fall ill and play no part in this battle. The complete force was 19,000-strong and heavily outnumbered the Royalists. It gathered at Bucklebury and moved towards the Royalists, seeking in particular to hold Clay Hill, overlooking Shaw House.

The Royalists placed a guard on Newbury Bridge, to stop an attack from the south. They already held Donnington Castle, and fortified Shaw House (where an existing earth bank in the garden was readily converted for defence), along with other properties on the north side of Newbury. Lord Astley was in command of the infantry. To the west, infantry led by Prince Maurice (King Charles' nephew) and some cavalry held the village of Speen. Just beyond the village they built an earthwork, stretching towards the Lambourn.

The Parliamentary army, with Manchester in charge, considered the idea of an attack from Clay Hill on Shaw House. The defences around Shaw House appeared strong, aided by the earthworks. It was decided to attack the Royalists from two sides at the same time: to do this, 12,000 troops were sent on a flanking march, to attack at Speen while Manchester and the rest of the army attacked from Clay Hill. The flanking march was led by Sir William Waller, with Philip Skippon leading the infantry, and Sir William Balfour and Oliver Cromwell as cavalry commanders. They put in a wide detour in an attempt to keep out of sight of Donnington Castle, covering 13 miles as they went out towards Hermitage, across to Chieveley, to North Heath (where they camped for part of the night near the Blue Boar/the Crab) and on to Boxford before coming in towards Speen from Stockcross.

The battle took place on Sunday, 27 October 1644, with the Royalists trying to hold their position against an attack on two flanks. In the attack on Speen, Waller was in command, with Cromwell's cavalry on the left.

The Royalists fought off the Parliamentary army to begin with, but then most of the defenders were driven back towards Newbury. King Charles, who was between Newbury and the village of Speen, was caught up in the fighting that followed, and was in some personal danger. A later Royalist account paints a vivid picture of King Charles (with the future Charles II, and some of his followers) attempting to rally troops who fled past him: '... A whole regiment of our Horse being stopped by His Majesty as they came down the lane from Speen, and commanded by him again into the field, very basely forsook him and ran into Newbury ...'. General Goring, leading Royalist cavalry, managed to block the attack and halt the rout.

Manchester sent in the Parliamentary forces to attack the strongly-defended Shaw House, but was driven off. One attack is reported as consisting of 1,200 cavalry and 3,000 infantry, with another 1,000 cavalry sent in support. Three times the Parliamentary forces came down the hill to attack, sometimes singing psalms as they came. Three times they were driven back with casualties, at times by cavalry, at times by infantry using the butt end of their muskets. Lieutenant Colonel Richard Page was the Royalist directly in charge of the house's defences, wounded in the action but receiving credit for driving the attackers so strongly away on one occasion that they were running back up the hill.

Neither side achieved a convincing victory, in spite of the superiority of numbers held by Parliament. Each commander had personal experience of the part of the battle which had gone worst for their side: King Charles was nearly captured; while Manchester had seen the casualties produced by the ineffective attacks on Shaw. However, Charles and the Royalists were the more vulnerable, and it was Charles who ordered a Royalist retreat. The army departed for Wallingford, and in spite of its vulnerability, it was not attacked. The King headed for Bath.

The Second Battle of Newbury could legitimately be described as a turning-point in the Civil War. Oliver Cromwell had taken part in the flanking march, and had seen the Parliamentary army effectively defeat part of the Royalists, yet (as he might see it) throw away its advantage. His experience of the battle was part of the motivation behind his wish to remove Manchester from command, which in turn was one of the factors which led to the Self-Denying Ordinance of 1645. This was intended to deprive existing generals of their commands, and so strengthen the army of Parliament. What emerged was the New Model Army; an army strong enough to win the Civil War for Parliament.

The Second Battle of Newbury was less bloody than the First. Royalist casualties were perhaps about 500, while there were more Parliamentary dead, with a total reaching anything up to about 1,000.

The Siege of Donnington Castle

Donnington Castle had been held for the Royalists since September 1643 by a small garrison under John Boys. He was appointed to take charge of the defences and was soon clearing hedges, trees and even houses within cannon-shot of the castle. His men set about creating additional defences, mounding earth around the castle and pushing in rows of nine-foot stakes. The aim was to extend the defensive area away from the castle walls, and to provide an effective platform for its artillery.

The defences were not put to the test for several months, and in the spring of 1644 the security of the castle received an extra boost when a Royalist army was stationed at Newbury for a month. By the end of May, however, with the army gone, the Parliamentary forces held all of south and east Berkshire except Donnington Castle. Even so, there was no immediate confrontation, with Boys' men making raids to gather stores and skirmishing frequently with the enemy.

In July, they made a provocative raid into Newbury on a Sunday, attempting to capture the Mayor and some of the town's more prominent citizens. In response, Lieutenant-General Middleton was sent to capture the castle with an army of more than 3,000 foot-soldiers and cavalry. On 14 July, the castle first came under cannon-fire and Middleton captured several musketeers who had been stationed in a barn near the castle. Then he drew up his forces for an assault, and demanded that Boys should surrender. Boys refused. A six-hour assault followed, in which – according to the Royalists – the attackers lost 100 men, including a Colonel, a Major and several other officers.

Middleton was then ordered to join a Parliamentary army in the West, and responsibility for taking the castle passed to the commander of the Parliamentary forces in Berkshire, Oxfordshire and Buckinghamshire, Major-General Brown. His adjutant-general, Colonel Jeremy Horton, gathered forces from Reading, Abingdon and Windsor, and started laying siege to the castle. He placed a battery of cannon on a field next to the road from Donnington to Speen and in less than two weeks it had destroyed three of the castle's eight towers and part of the curtain wall. Horton then demanded that Boys should surrender, but Boys again refused.

The battery was moved to the Snelsmore side of the castle, but Boys' forces staged a night attack on their trenches, killing many soldiers

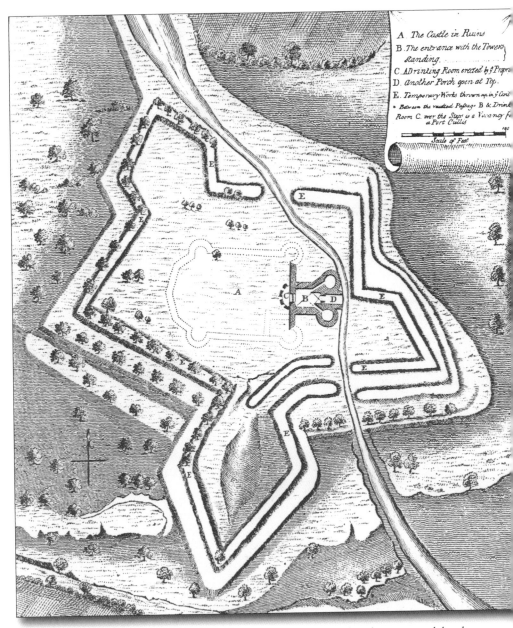

A. *The Castle in Ruins*
B. *The entrance with the Towers standing.*
C. *A Drinting Room erected by y Propr*
D. *Another Porch open at Top.*
E. *Temporary Works thrown up in y Civil*
• *Between the vaulted Passage B & Drink*
Room C. over the Steps is a Vacancy f
a Port Cullis

Scale of Feet

A plan of Donnington Castle showing the defensive earthworks constructed by the Royalist defenders.

including a Colonel and the chief cannoneer, and captured arms and ammunition. Nevertheless, the bombardment continued for another seven days, making 19 in total. In all, over 1,000 rounds had been fired at the castle. The timely arrival of the King and a Royalist army saved the castle from further destruction. On 22 October 1644, King Charles knighted John Boys for his conduct of the defence.

Five days later came the Second Battle of Newbury. The day after the battle, the Parliamentary army surrounded the ruined castle. Once more, they demanded that Sir John Boys surrender, saying that they would not leave one stone upon another. 'If so, I am not bound to repair it,' was Boys' reply. Twice more they asked him to surrender, offering to let his men take their arms with them and even the cannon. Boys refused again. He was not just stubbornly defending a ruin. Left in his keeping after the battle were the Great Seal, various pieces of gold and silver, some Royal decrees, and the King's Crown.

In spite of his firm answers to the Parliamentary army, Boys felt very vulnerable and sent messages pleading for relief, saying that the Parliamentary generals Manchester and Waller were in Newbury with an army approaching 8,000 men; in the castle's defence were 250 men and officers.

The attackers tried an assault. It failed, and the officer leading it was killed. Then, to add to Boys' luck, the Parliamentary generals seem to have fallen out among themselves, and there was no further attack.

Thirteen days after the battle, the King and his army returned to Donnington, relieving the castle. The King spent that night (9 November 1644) there and the next morning the army was drawn up on the north side of the castle, with many of the light cannon which had been left after the battle. From Snelsmore, they marched to Winterbourne, and then on through Boxford and Lambourn, taking with them the Crown and other valuables. It was the beginning of a quiet time for the castle, which can only be explained in terms of the national politics of the Civil War.

Nearly a year later, in November 1645, Colonel Dalbier arrived in Newbury with Parliamentary forces from Berkshire, Oxfordshire and Buckinghamshire, and was met by infantry and cavalry from Hampshire, Sussex, Surrey and even Kent. He had overwhelming numbers, while Boys was still guarding his ruin with about 200 men. Dalbier heard that the King and a Royalist army were at Oxford, and promptly moved his men out to Aldermaston. When he returned in December, he found that houses in and around Donnington had been burnt, on Boys' orders. Still there was no confrontation. The castle's defences were strengthened, and

Boys made sallies against Parliamentary troops in Burghclere, Woodhay, Greenham and Kintbury.

Not until March 1646 did Dalbier begin his siege. He moved up his forces to face the castle, and called on Boys to surrender. Boys asked for three days to get orders from the King at Oxford, but the same night Dalbier's men started raising earthworks on the east side of the castle which would command the gateway. These Boys decided to attack. Cavalry and foot-soldiers, led by Captain Donne, fell on them, killing about 80 and taking 63 prisoners. They also captured four flags, weapons and working tools.

Dalbier's men, in force, re-took the trenches and the next day planted a large cannon or 'mortar piece' on the earthworks. It was highly destructive for its time, with explosive shells, and when it started shelling the castle the effect was immediate. Within hours, the remains of the castle were shattered. Now Dalbier had Boys and his defenders at his mercy, but wrote again demanding that he surrender. Boys again asked for permission to send two officers to Oxford. This time Dalbier agreed, and the King's reply was that Boys should surrender the castle on the best terms he could get and then, if possible, march his men to Oxford to join the Royalist army there.

The terms of the surrender were agreed on 30 March 1646, in a field on the east side of the castle, and the terms were surprisingly lenient. The defenders were allowed to leave the castle with drums beating, flags flying and bullets in their mouths – as if ready for action – on 1 April. They were allowed to go to their own homes, providing they agreed not to take up arms against Parliament again, and providing they released their prisoners. Left in the castle were six cannon, about 20 barrels of gunpowder and other ammunition. The defenders numbered between 150 and 200. Since the time of the first attack, in July 1644, the castle had held out for a year and nine months. In the face of such overwhelming odds, Boys had mounted a stubborn resistance.

The Later 17th century

The most striking building which houses Camp Hopson in Northbrook Street is dated 1663, shortly after the Restoration of the Monarchy. This was built for George Cowslade, mayor of Newbury in 1663, who met King Charles II when he toured the sites of the battles of Newbury. Other 17th-century buildings include the Manor House in London Road, the Monument pub in Northbrook Street, and a taxi office/hairdresser in Cheap Street (nos. 49-50).

The 17th-century Monument pub, named after the Monument to the Great Fire of London, can still be seen in Northbrook Street.

Several almshouses were founded in Newbury in the late 17th century. The largest of these were the Raymonds Almshouses, established before 1676 by Philip Jemmet and further endowed by his son-in-law and daughter, Sir Jonathan and Lady Raymond. Jemmet's foundation was originally for twelve almspeople, and the number was later increased to 22. The almshouses were at first on the west side of Argyle Road, but they were moved to the east side of Newtown Road in 1796 (near Fair Close, the best-known section now), with a later range erected north of Derby Road.

Coxedd's (or Coxhead's) Almshouses were founded in 1690 by the will of Francis Coxhead and consisted of two almshouses at 15-16 West Mills. Pearce's Almshouses were founded in 1671 by the will of Thomas Pearce, and consisted of two almshouses next door at 17-18 West Mills, near the swing bridge. Although the buildings in West Mills survive, in the early 1880s the two almshouse charities merged, all four almshouses

A 17th-century building in Cheap Street (49-50), still playing a useful role in the life of the town.

in West Mills were sold, and they were replaced by new almshouses in Enborne Road.

Nonconformity

In the later 17th century, Newbury saw a flourishing of Protestant groups which did not wish to be part of the Church of England, the Nonconformists. One of the leading figures locally was the Rev. Benjamin Woodbridge, who had been Rector. There were already Nonconformists in Newbury at the beginning of the Civil War, and the sympathies of many of the churchgoers were with the Puritans. This led to riots over the election of a churchwarden in 1664, followed by arrests. William Milton and a number of others were sent to London for trial. After this event, the number of practising Nonconformists in Newbury was given as only 40.

Pearce's Almshouses were founded in 1671 by the will of Thomas Pearce and are still standing in West Mills. (inset) This carving that used to be above the entrance to the almhouses now adorns almshouses off Enborne Road.

Rev. Benjamin Woodbridge officially left the Church of England in 1662, soon after the Restoration, and many of his congregation went with him. They continued united until after his death in 1684. Then they split into two distinct congregations, the Presbyterians and the Independents.

The Presbyterians moved their meeting house to the Waterside Chapel in 1697. This old chapel was picturesque with its mellow red-brick walls, and gabled roofs. The first Minister there was William Taylor, who was succeeded about 1700 by James Peirce. Later the Unitarian Chapel, it was demolished in 1960 and replaced by the Waterside Youth Centre.

The first Minister for the Independents was the Rev. Benjamin Merriman, who was ordained to the office in 1686, aged 24. He was a Newbury man, and had studied at Oxford. Shortly afterwards, they moved to a barn in Cromwell Place, where the Independents built their first chapel in 1717 (later becoming the Congregationalists, who in turn merged with the Presbyterians to create the current United Reformed Church).

The Quakers held large meetings in Newbury in the 1670s and 1680s, and had become established in the town by 1683. Their first meeting house stood behind the street frontage in Bartholomew Street.

A Baptist congregation in Newbury existed in the 1640s, although it first appears officially in a return of 1669, with a reference to one small congregation of 'Anabaptists'. Their meeting place is given as the house of Thomas Merriman (probably in Cheap Street). However, the first regular Baptist minister was a Mr Peter James, and by then the Baptists met in the upper room of a house in Northbrook Street, recorded as the house of Mr Jabez Hill, grocer (now part of Camp Hopson). There they continued until a meeting house was built in Northcroft Lane, licensed for religious worship in 1702.

Chapter 5

The Eighteenth Century: Georgian Newbury

The 18th century was one of extensive changes in transport locally, with the building of a waterway from Reading to Newbury, and the start of its extension to the west, as the Kennet and Avon Canal. The Bath Road was rebuilt and systematically maintained as a toll-road, servicing an area which benefited greatly from the 'coaching era'.

The Kennet Navigation

With poor roads at the beginning of the century, there was a clear advantage to towns which had access to water transport, substantially cutting the cost of carrying bulk goods. Alterations were made to the River Kennet, including the creation of some new canal-like sections, in order to make a commercial waterway from Reading to Newbury. For this 'Kennet Navigation' an Act of Parliament was needed, which was put forward in 1708 but met with strong opposition from Reading. Water-carried goods had been unloaded at Reading to be transported overland to Newbury and into Wiltshire; the consequence of creating a waterway to Newbury would be to take away jobs in Reading. After a fight, the Kennet Navigation Act was passed in 1715, and work started on the locks needed to cope with the 41 metre (134 ft) difference in level between Newbury and Reading. These had slanting turf-covered sides, rather than the vertical brick chambers which became familiar later. Work was overseen by engineer John Hore.

Reading continued to resist. In 1719 a 300-strong mob attacked the work under progress, causing considerable damage: among the mob was the Mayor of Reading. Eventually work was completed and the Kennet Navigation opened in 1723, allowing barges to travel from the Thames at Reading to Newbury. A large basin for loading and unloading barges was constructed at Newbury Wharf, and Newbury became an important inland port, servicing not just the town but the whole area to the west, into Wiltshire. The main goods carried were bulk goods, where water transport offered a practical alternative to the roads. Corn, flour, malt and cheese went from Newbury to London; with coals, iron, pine and other heavy goods in return.

Originally barges were expected to sail the waterway, but the need for a towpath became clear and it was completed in May 1724. In the 1760s the locks were enlarged to take the 128-ton 'Newbury' barges, significantly bigger than narrow boats (109 ft long, 17 ft beam, and 3 ft 6 inch draught when loaded with 110 tons).

It was the success of the Kennet Navigation, and the trade associated with it, which contributed to prosperity among a section of Newbury society in the 18th century, and it was this period which saw the building of some grand houses in and around the town, which still make a strong contribution to Newbury's visual character.

Later in the 18th century came the technology to build new waterways without needing to follow rivers for their water supply, creating the true canals. The river navigations were extremely prosperous, and in Newbury there were suggestions of extending the Kennet Navigation to Hungerford, then into Wiltshire, and finally right across southern England, by joining up the Kennet and the Avon navigations, a solution called for in 1788 at a meeting in Hungerford. This led in 1794 to the Kennet and Avon Canal Act, passed very quickly. The work was planned and supervised by the engineer John Rennie. Construction started in October 1794 at both ends, at Bradford-on-Avon and at Newbury, and the first contracts were for 15-mile stretches at each end. Newbury Lock is thought to have been the first lock completed. In June 1797 the canal opened from Newbury to Kintbury. In October it opened to Hungerford. Now Britain was involved in the French Revolutionary wars, and money became a problem, holding up the construction and pushing back the completion date. The canal west into Wiltshire was completed in the 18th century, but the canal as a whole took longer, and eventually opened in 1810.

Barges were made in Newbury not just for the local waterways, but for a much wider market. They would be loaded with timber which could be sold, along with the barge, in London or further afield.

The Bath Road

Until the 18th century, English roads were poor at the best of times, and many became almost impassable in the winter. Then the road engineers appeared, paid for with income drawn from turning the major roads into toll roads, otherwise known as turnpike roads. The Bath Road was the earliest major road to be reconstructed, servicing the regular transfer of the wealthiest section of society between London and Bath, and back again. It was divided into sections, each section having a 'Turnpike Trust' which employed an engineer to improve the line and surface of the road. Each Trust's income came from annually auctioning the right to collect the tolls.

One local toll gate was on the Bath Road near the junction with Turnpike Road, by the roundabout where Tull Road now leaves the A4 (Thatcham gate); this was on the Theale (Puntfield) to Newbury (Speenhamland) section of the road, made a turnpike from 1728. The auction for the right to collect tolls here raised over £400 a year in the 1780s. On the west side of Newbury the toll house was an attractive building with battlements near Halfway (Hoe Benham gate) which survived until demolition in 1966. This was on the Speenhamland to Marlborough section of the road, which was first made a turnpike or toll road by an Act of Parliament in 1726. As with Thatcham gate, the auction for the right to collect tolls here was normally held at the Globe Inn in Newbury, a large inn on the site of the modern Lloyds Bank. In the 1780s the auction raised over £600 each year.

Because of the name 'Turnpike Road', there has been some confusion over the route of the London/Bath Road into Newbury. This followed more or less the same line as the modern A4. Turnpike Road was given its name in 1934 because it led to and from the former toll house, which stood on the A4 until the 1960s.

Nationally, the two names best known for road improvements were McAdam and Telford. John Loudan McAdam publishing best-selling books on road-mending, and became closely involved in changes to the Bath Road, appointed in 1815 as Surveyor-General of the Bristol Roads. In 1819 Mr George Botham, the landlord of the George and Pelican Inn at Newbury, told Parliament that there had been a great improvement in the road between Marlborough and Twyford (east of Reading), under McAdam's direction.

The coaching era

In the 18th century, improvements to road-making were accompanied by increasing traffic, and it was a struggle to keep ahead. In 1767 a writer to the *Reading Mercury* referred to problems with mud and flooding, and difficulties presented by narrow stretches, especially near Ham Mills (now by B & Q). There the road was dangerous for two coaches to pass, as it was narrow and had ditches on both sides, one very deep.

In spite of problems with the surface of the road, the speed of travel steadily increased. In 1752 the 'Flying Coach' was introduced from Newbury to London, 'flying' because of its speed: it only took twelve hours to get to London. It started from the White Hart Inn in the Market Place (now Gardner Leader solicitors). The original advertisement spoke of the 'Newbury four wheel'd stage chaise, made with steel springs, to carry four passengers at ten shillings each to or from London. Sets out from the White Hart Inn, in Newbury, on Mondays, Wednesdays, and Fridays at six o'clock in the morning to the Saracen's Head, Snow Hill; and returns from thence on Tuesdays, Thursdays and Saturdays: and will be at their quarters each evening by six.'

Coaching inns flourished in Newbury, especially in Speenhamland, the part of Newbury which was then in the parish of Speen, and through which the London to Bath Road passed. From west to east, these included (not all open at the same time) the Castle, the Bacon Arms (previously the Maidenhead Inn), the Chequers, the Bear, the George and Pelican (a large and famous inn, behind the present Clock Tower), the Cross Keys, the Lamb and Flag, the Star, and the Kings Arms (better known later as the Dower House). The whole of 'society' passed along the Bath Road in the 18th century, staying the night, stopping for food or simply changing horses. More inns could be found in Newbury itself, some servicing the north-south roads.

The buildings of the George and Pelican still stand in Broadway and stretch a little east (towards the Robin Hood roundabout). The eastern end of this range formed the entrance to the Pelican stables. These stretched extensively to the rear, and at one time had accommodation for 300 horses. Like all coaching inns it provided food, but gained a reputation as an expensive place to eat. James Quinn, a well-known actor in the mid-18th century, reputedly scratched a verse on one of its windows:

'The famous inn at Speenhamland
That stands below the hill
May well be called the Pelican
From its enormous bill.'

The hill was Speen Hill (now the Old Bath Road), home of the Castle

Thames Court (formerly York House), part of the old George and Pelican, is one of Newbury's finest buildings.

Inn. While the concentration of inns was in Speenhamland, there were others in the town, some serving the north-south routes. The principal inns were the Jack in Northbrook Street (Marks & Spencer), the Globe on the south side of Newbury Bridge (Lloyds Bank) and the White Hart in the Market Place (Gardner Leader, but still with its 'White Hart' sign).

Many trades servicing the coaching industry flourished: those looking after the horses, the carriages and the saddlery; those providing hospitality to the travellers; and others who responded to the wealth of many of the travellers, such as the local watch and clock industry. There were over a hundred clockmakers in Newbury, Speen and Shaw between 1680 and 1840, some of them producing very high quality work.

The mail coaches

The national network of mail coaches began on the Bath Road, with coaches running to a strict timetable which in many ways anticipated the railways. Previously the mail was carried by post-boys on horseback, sometimes rather unpredictably. The idea of using coaches came from John Palmer, a theatre manager who organised the first mail coach run in August 1784. Fresh horses and the mails were ready for when the coach stopped. It was also exempt from tolls; the sound of the horn from the mail-coach meant that the turnpike keeper had to raise the barrier, and the coach could go through without pausing. The first run proved a success, and a regular service started days later.

A schedule from this period shows coaches leaving the Post Office in London at 8 pm and stopping in Piccadilly and Brentford, before arriving at Thatcham at 2.45 am, with a 20-minute stop before going on through Newbury to Marlborough, Calne, Bath and Bristol, which it reached at 11 am. The mail coach in the opposite direction set off from Bristol at 4 pm, reached Thatcham at 11.55 pm, when there was again a 20-minute stop before going on to reach London at 7 am. The regular mail stop in Thatcham was at the King's Head, run by Edward and Mary Fromont.

At the height of the coaching era (c.1780–1840) the best coachmen were an elite class of workers, who needed to be literate and numerate. In the early 19th century several chose to live in the newly-built houses of Shaw Road. The coaching days sometimes present a picturesque image, but in bad weather the conditions were atrocious and much hardship was suffered by both passengers and horses. Keeping to the schedule was difficult and there were many complaints, as can be gathered from an inscription on the gravestone of a coachman buried in Speen churchyard:

In memory of James Murray
late Bath coachman
who died 20th May 1796
aged 46 years
Tho' while on earth I did remain
I was reproached and scorned by men
But now am numbered with the saints
And saf'd of all my long complaints.

Newbury Bridge

Newbury Bridge, at the heart of the town, was built in the 18th century to replace a series of wooden bridges, some swept away by floods. In spite of appearances, it is a three-arched structure, with the outer two arches incorporated in the adjoining buildings. It was built by Newbury-based master-builder James Clarke. The first stone was laid on 28 July 1769, and it was completed in 1772. The shelters at each corner were originally

Newbury Bridge: the 18th-century stone bridge replacing previous timber bridges.

free-standing, and the balusters are made of metal, not stone. It is said to have cost £700.

The bridge pre-dates the canal, so there is no provision for a towpath. Boats going upstream had to moor just below the bridge and the towing rope was floated back to them through the bridge, using a float kept at Newbury Lock. Going downstream was not easy either. Boats needed to gain momentum quickly on leaving Newbury Lock, to steer cleanly through the narrow bridge. Horses were taken through the tunnel to one side, across Northbrook Street, and back down to the canal again.

As well as Newbury Bridge, James Clarke was also responsible for the now-demolished Mansion House nearby in Mansion House Street, built in 1742. This served for a time as Newbury's town hall, provided a venue for 'Assemblies' of the local gentry (in Jane Austen style, with dancing and card games), and was used for theatrical and other entertainments. The basement of the building was fitted with extensive and costly cooking equipment for the Mayor's Inaugural Dinner. Functions were held on the first floor, built over open arches, and the 'shambles' underneath was used by stallholders for the sale of meat, butter and poultry.

St Nicolas' House, an 18th-century building in the style of James Clarke of Newbury.

The Dower House (formerly the King's Arms inn), sadly demolished in the 1950s.

Clarke also built the home of the Head family at 91–92 Northbrook Street, and several other 18th-century houses in Newbury are attributed to him, including St Nicolas House in West Mills, no. 5 Wharf Street (next to the Hog's Head), and 44 London Road (Clarendon House), which was part of the old King's Arms.

★★

Daniel Defoe, author of *Robinson Crusoe*, wrote about Newbury in the 1720s: 'This town of Newbery is an ancient clothing town, though now little of that part remains to it; but it retains still a manufacturing genius, and the people are generally employed in making shalloons, a kind of stuff which, though it be used only for the lining and insides of men's clothes (for women use but little of it, nor men for anything but as above), yet it becomes so generally worn, both at home and abroad, that it is increased to a manufacturer by itself ...'.

As the century continued, however, even the manufacture of this poor material shrank, and the cloth industry went into terminal decline in this area. There were many causes, among them the rise of industrial cloth production in the north of England.

In 1766 rising food prices and local poverty reached a crisis. A large number of people gathered in the Market Place on an August market day to protest at the high price of bread. They upset sacks of corn and several traders' stalls, and then targeted the houses of two unpopular tradesmen. In an attempt to pacify the crowd, the bakers reduced the price of bread by 2d with promises of a further reduction the following week. But the crowd then marched on Shaw Mill, breaking windows, throwing flour into the river, and causing more damage. Other local mills were also attacked, several people were injured and one was killed. Troops were called and a number of arrests were made. A public subscription was raised in Newbury to supply bread to the poor at 9d a gallon loaf, and the millers agreed to grind their wheat free of charge. Others throughout the area also made arrangements to supply the poor with wheat at a reduced price. Two of those identified as ringleaders of the bread riot were tried at the Assizes, and sentenced to transportation.

As in other parts of the country, Newbury still suffered with periodic bouts of smallpox during the 18th century. Apart from those who died, it could have a serious effect on business in the town when visitors stayed away. There was a bad epidemic in 1753, and another which started in 1767 and ran into the following year. In March 1768 Speen's vicar, churchwardens, overseer of the poor and other prominent individuals in Speenhamland took out an advertisement in the *Reading Mercury* to make a public assurance that after visiting every house, they could not now find anyone who had the disease.

The celebrated astronomer Francis Baily was born in Newbury in 1774, although he is better known for his association with Thatcham. His parents lived in a large house on the west side of Northbrook Street which later became the Liberal Club, demolished in the 1960s and replaced by Brook House. He was a founder and several times President of the Royal Astronomical Society, and gave his name to 'Baily's beads'.

Sandleford Priory and Mrs Montagu

Sandleford Priory was transformed in the 18th century, creating the imposing building now used as St Gabriel's School. The house and surrounding land were leased by Edward Montagu, the wealthy owner of coal-mines in the north-east. His wife Elizabeth became a focus for a literary and artistic circle, hosting large assemblies or 'conversation parties' at her London home, where guests included Samuel Johnson, Sir Joshua Reynolds, Edmund Burke, and David Garrick. The regulars at these events became known as 'bluestockings,' with Elizabeth Montagu as 'the

Queen of the bluestockings.' She was a woman who visited Donnington Castle because of the possible link to Geoffrey Chaucer, and was disappointed when she found it being used to house pheasants and partridges, rather than being appreciated for its literary connection. She was a literary figure herself and is now best known for her extensive collection of letters.

Sandleford was her retreat into the countryside, away from city life. In 1780, five years after her husband's death, she commissioned architect James Wyatt to draw up plans to remodel Sandleford in a more Gothic style. The main front, seen from the A339, is Wyatt's 18th-century creation. If any of the main medieval building is left, it may be embedded in some of the thick walls which remain. Mrs Montagu's new bedroom and dressing room were on the first floor, facing south, towards the River Enborne. At the rear, originally separate, was the priory's chapel. This had not been used for services for many years. Wyatt extensively remodelled it for Mrs Montagu to form a large dining room, removing obvious signs of its religious past. She wrote that it had been '…taken from the owls, the bats, the rats and mice to be dedicated to the sober use of sober society, and a temperate dinner preceded and concluded by a grace …'. Linking the chapel to the main building is the oval Drawing Room, an impressive construction added by Wyatt in a very classical, Adamish style.

The changes to the house took several years to complete, and Mrs Montagu also brought in 'Capability' Brown to remodel the surrounding

Sandleford Priory, an 18th-century 'Gothick' house.

landscape. Sandleford has been described as Brown's last great commission before his death in 1782.

Mrs Montagu put some local labour to work on the grounds, describing them as 'poor weavers who by the decay of our manufacture at Newbury are void of employment and, not having been trained to the business of agriculture are not dexterous at the rake and pitchfork, but the plain digging and driving wheel barrows they can perform and are very glad to get their daily subsistence.'

★★

Another 18th-century Gothic building close to Newbury is Donnington Grove, designed in 1763 for James Pettit Andrews by John Chute of The Vyne, near Basingstoke. Chute was a member of Horace Walpole's Committee of Taste for Strawberry Hill. Some of his designs for Donnington Grove survive at The Vyne, drawn by the carpenter and builder John Hobcraft, who was also the architect for Padworth House. While less imposing, St Mary's House, on London Road opposite the top of Park Way, was refronted in a similar style and is probably also by Chute.

Almshouses continued to multiply in the town, including some in Cheap Street, Newtown Road, Northcroft Lane, and West Mills. Three almshouses in West Mills were established by the will of Thomas Hunt, dated June 1727. They were originally for three poor widows, and were rebuilt in 1817. That building survives, end-on to West Mills, with the blank oval which used to carry a dated inscription facing the road.

By the will of Benjamin Robinson, in September 1754, three cottages were purchased in Bartholomew Street for use as almshouses; in 1764 they were sold, and replaced by three cottages leased in Northcroft Lane.

Next to the post office in the middle of Newbury were Kimber's Almshouses, a group of twelve which survived until the 1950s. They were created by John Kimber, who was Mayor of Newbury in 1758. In his will of 1790, he left money for the creation of almshouses for six men and six women. He died in 1793 and by January 1794 his trustees had purchased a site on the east side of Cheap Street, close to the Market Place. There the almshouses were built, completed in 1795. Kimber also left a weekly income for the residents and money for clothes. In the late 1930s replacement almshouses were built in Kennet Road, and the buildings next to the post office stood empty during the 1940s and into the 1950s, when they were demolished.

At Fair Close, at right angles to Newtown Road, is a terrace of twelve houses called the Lower Raymond Almshouses. They were built in 1796, and the date still appears in a scroll on the centre on the terrace. These were part of a charity originally founded in 1676 by Philip Jemmett, and involving his grandson Jemmett Raymond.

Campaign against slavery

At the height of the slave trade Newbury residents organised a petition to Parliament, calling for an end to a practice which 'is disgraceful to our national character, and by which we become the instruments of misery to innumerable multitudes of our fellow creatures.' The year was 1788, one year before the outbreak of the French Revolution. On 7 April a public meeting was called in Newbury Town Hall (i.e. the Mansion House), with Newbury's Mayor John Hasker and many burgesses (members of the Corporation) among those present.

They came together to oppose the slave trade, and unanimously agreed on the text of a petition to be presented to the House of Commons immediately. It stated that the Mayor, aldermen, burgesses and inhabitants of Newbury were 'deeply impressed with the injustice and inhumanity of the Slave Trade,' and called for it to be stopped by any practical means. They petitioned the House of Commons to take 'such measures as shall to your wisdom and humanity appear best calculated for bringing to a speedy end the horrors of a commerce which is disgraceful to our national character…'.

A vote of thanks was made to the Mayor for agreeing to call the public meeting. Thanks were also offered to Newbury Baptist minister the Rev. James Bicheno, who had himself apparently been sold into slavery in the U.S. state of Virginia and since gaining his freedom and training as a minister had been involved in the campaign for the abolition of the slave trade. Bicheno was probably the author of an advertisement which had appeared in the *Reading Mercury* the previous month, in the form of a passionate address 'To the Inhabitants of Newbury,' in which he said: 'Hundreds of men, women and children are crowded into the hold of a ship, exposed to the despotic will, the lust and cruelty of unfeeling seamen; and all this is aggravated by the dreadful uncertainty which lies before them. Multitudes perish on their passage; those who survive are sold as cattle, to be slaves for life …'.

The author noted that others were already protesting against 'this odious and guilty traffic in human flesh.' The Newbury petition was presented in the House on Commons on Thursday, 24 April, less than three weeks after the public meeting in Newbury. The Commons decided to take no action at all after the petition was read; in parliamentary language, it 'was ordered to lie on the table.' It was one of over 100 petitions protesting about slavery presented to Parliament during 1788, and formed part of the first national campaign organised by the Society for the Abolition of the Slave Trade.

The Speenhamland System

In 1795, a new welfare system began with a meeting at the Pelican Inn in Speenhamland, just by the Clock Tower. This was the Speenhamland System, which established a new system of benefits or 'poor relief' by subsidising low wages with taxpayers' money (varying the subsidy in line with the price of bread). The decision at the meeting, held on 6 May, applied only to Berkshire but the idea was taken up and spread widely (with variations), and it became the model system especially for southern and central England.

The Speenhamland System was agreed at a meeting of Berkshire magistrates, chaired by Charles Dundas of Barton Court, Kintbury. The meeting was called in response to the economic hardship felt by local labourers at the time, during the French revolutionary wars. The magistrates were originally expected to fix a minimum wage and, while they agreed that 'the present state of the poor does require further assistance', the meeting opted instead for a top-up paid from the rates (the local tax). They decided that when a gallon loaf (8 lb 11 oz) cost a shilling, then every poor man should have for his support three shillings a week, and that if his wages fell short of that, the rest of the amount should be provided from the rates. If the loaf rose to 1s 4d, then the minimum income should be 4 shillings (still three times the price of the loaf). Additional amounts were set out for his wife and children (set at half as much and rising less rapidly). In other words, each man must have the equivalent of three gallon loaves a week, and his wife and each child one and a half.

The national importance of this system lay in its widespread adoption as a model, albeit with variations. As one historian wrote: '…never before had a single scale, which prevented trouble-making variations between parishes and individuals, been so rapidly and widely adopted. Some counties still favoured different, and usually less generous, scales of their own, but the principle was almost universally accepted …'.

Other historians argue that the considerable variations make a nonsense of describing it as a single 'system'. Nevertheless, this was a change of historical importance.

Its structure created its own problems: there was little incentive for employers to pay decent wages if whatever they paid would be topped up from the rates; and the national cost rose steadily. As part of the 'Old Poor Law', its defects provided ammunition for those involved in setting up the workhouse system (in the 'Oliver Twist' sense, with the intimidating Union workhouses) in the 1830s.

★★

One Newbury business founded in the 18th century was Dreweatts, the auctioneers, estate agents and valuers, recently swallowed up by Carter Jonas. The firm was started by Thomas Davis in 1759, when he moved from Abingdon and opened in the Market Place, advertising himself at first as 'Brazier, Upholster and Appraiser'. In 1770 he handled the leases of two farms on the Sydmonton estate and from that time on, held numerous sales of farm stock around the district. The business continued in the Davis family until the 1880s, when Thomas Dreweatt joined.

Another 18th-century Newbury business was engineering firm Plenty Ltd. Although established in Southampton in 1779 by William Plenty, the firm moved to Newbury in 1790. It occupied the Eagle Ironworks between Bartholomew Street and Cheap Street (part of the site now occupied by the Kennet Centre), with access from Cheap Street. In its early years the concentration was on agricultural machinery and the items produced included harrows, chaff cutters, feeding troughs for livestock and water carts. In 1815 it patented a special design of plough, a major step forward at a time when much of the countryside was being enclosed and the size of fields was increasing. It also made sluices for the Kennet and Avon Canal.

The Revolutionary wars against France gave rise to fears of invasion in the 1790s, which prompted national preparations for defence. In April 1798 a meeting was held at the Mansion House to form an 'Armed Association' for the defence of Newbury and the surrounding area. The result was the creation of volunteer cavalry and infantry, the latter called the 'Newbury, Shaw and Speen Volunteer Infantry,' which was among the volunteer forces for Berkshire reviewed by King George III in 1799.

Chapter 6

Nineteenth-Century Newbury

The coaching era continued into the 19th century, with many of the most prominent and wealthiest individuals passing through Newbury. The opportunities presented may have played a part in the opening of Newbury Theatre in 1802. The theatre stood at the end of a square set back from Oxford Street, close to the coaching inns along the Bath Road, with a grand façade which appears in engravings from the period. Edmund Keen, John Philip Kemble, Mrs Jordan and Miss Bruton were among those who appeared there. The theatre was opened by Henry Thornton, who previously ran a less imposing theatre in Northcroft Lane, and it was then run by his son-in-law, Edward Barnett. It closed in the 1840s and was converted to other uses before it was demolished in 1976.

The Newbury Coat

Industry had developed dramatically during the 18th century and this is reflected in a celebrated event in Newbury in 1811, the making of the Newbury Coat. Sir John Throckmorton of Buckland near Faringdon bet 1,000 guineas (£1,050) that a coat could be made in one day, between sunrise and sunset. The wool would start the day on the backs of sheep, and the day would end with him sitting down to dinner in a finished coat made from that wool.

The appointed day was Tuesday, 25 June 1811. At 5 am the work began, with two sheep sheared and the wool given to Mr John Coxeter of Greenham Mills in Mill Lane. The task at Greenham Mills was to make a type of cloth called a hunting kersey. The wool was spun into yarn. The yarn was prepared for the loom by being spooled, warped and loomed. John Coxeter's own son John took charge of weaving the three-and-a-half yards of cloth needed. Then came the processes to give the cloth its finish:

Newbury Market Place c.1800, from part of a picture by Thomas Rowlandson.

it was burred, milled and rowed, before being dyed a colour known as 'Wellington'. It was then dried, sheared and pressed, and the finished cloth was ready by 4 pm, after eleven hours.

The cloth was handed to Newbury tailor Mr Isaac White, who measured Sir John for the coat and whose son James cut it out and made the coat within two hours and twenty minutes. At 6.20 pm Mr Coxeter handed the finished coat to Sir John Throckmorton. People had gathered in Newbury throughout the day, and Sir John appeared wearing the coat before a crowd estimated at 5,000 people, before sitting down to a dinner provided by Mr Coxeter, with nearly 40 'gentlemen'. The crowd did not miss out. Both sheep were roasted and one was given to the workers of Greenham Mills, together with 120 gallons of strong beer, while the other was for the rest of the crowd. Church bells rang during the day to mark the occasion.

The original Newbury Coat has been on display for many years at the Throckmorton family home of Coughton Court in Warwickshire, now run by the National Trust.

The Swing Riots

By 1830 life had become very hard for agricultural workers across a large part of southern England, including Berkshire. Many parishes in West Berkshire had seen common fields enclosed, a process which increased the number of farm labourers dependent on others for their employment, and a proportional fall in the number of small yeomen farmers. There was also a lack of piece-work such as spinning, which had provided extra income for small farmers. And, most recently, the introduction of steam-powered threshing machines had removed the staple work available during the winter, that of threshing corn by hand.

In late 1830 agricultural riots started in Kent and reached Berkshire in November. Labourers gathered in groups and moved from farm to farm. In West Berkshire they had three main aims: they set out to smash all the threshing machines, secure an increase in wages, and take food or cash from farmers, as an instant welfare payment.

Almost every village in the area was affected, with six main centres across the district: Yattendon, Thatcham, Speen, Kintbury, Hungerford and Lambourn. It was the Thatcham group which started first, meeting on 15 November. Several mobs roamed the area on an almost daily basis from then until 24 November, and many threshing machines were destroyed. On just one day, for example, 23 November, threshing machines were destroyed at Basildon, Boxford, Benham, Eastbury, East Garston, Enborne, Great Shefford, Hamstead Marshall, Hungerford, Inkpen, Kintbury, Lambourn, Streatley, Welford, West Woodhay and Wickham.

Soldiers were called out to deal with the riots, and many arrests were made. A newspaper account of a group of Berkshire trials mentions 138 prisoners, the majority of whom were charged with riotously assembling, and destroying threshing machines and other property. The sentence against many of the rioters was one of transportation. Three people were sentenced to death, but in two of these cases the sentences were commuted to transportation. The exception was the leader of the Kintbury men, William Winterbourne who was executed at Winchester.

★★

Reaction to the Swing Riots quickly led to pressure for changes to the welfare system, the 'Old Poor Law', and its replacement by a system of large and intimidating workhouses which would deter the poor from claiming welfare unless they were desperate. This came into effect with the Poor Law Amendment Act of 1834, and the Newbury Workhouse in Newtown Road was one of those built following the Act.

The Newbury Board of Guardians met in 1835 to begin work, the foundation stone was laid in Newtown Road in August and the Newbury Workhouse itself was completed in June 1836. Workhouse buildings, like that at Newbury, were deliberately built as large, grim, prison-like structures, as part of their intended deterrent effect. A separate 22-bed infirmary was completed in March 1837, and the workhouse was first extended in the late 1840s. It was run by a master and matron, responsible to the Newbury Board of Guardians, who in turn answered to the Poor Law Commissioners in London. It was a 'Union' workhouse, because the workhouse was built by and served a union of local parishes. The parishes in the Newbury Union were Newbury, Boxford, Brimpton, Chieveley, Enborne, Greenham, Hamstead Marshall, Leckhampstead, Midgham, Newtown, Shaw-cum-Donnington, Speen, Thatcham, Wasing, Welford, Winterborne and Woolhampton

The workhouse system generally became more humane as the 19th century progressed; in the 20th century, Newbury workhouse became Sandleford Hospital. Sandleford was incorporated into the National Health Service on its formation in the 1940s, and continued for many years as a hospital with an emphasis on geriatric patients and maternity.

Rotten Borough

The 18th and early 19th centuries was the period of the Rotten Boroughs, when the Corporation which ran Newbury was not organised for the benefit of the town as a whole, but largely for its own members. Newbury was an oligarchy, and its members had their hands on considerable charity money and assets, which became intertwined in complex confusion. Some charity activities, such as providing schools, either stopped or depended heavily on new voluntary contributions. Much of the charity money vanished without trace, including considerable sums which formed part of the Kendrick charity bequest.

When it came to lighting, paving and cleaning the town of Newbury, residents could not turn to the Corporation. Instead they set up their own Improvement Commission, raised their own money and got an act passed in Parliament in 1825, 'An Act for lighting, watching, paving, cleansing and improving the streets, highways and places within the Borough, Town and Parish of Newbury and the Tithing or Hamlet of Speenhamland in the parish of Speen in the county of Berks.'

Following the Great Reform Act of 1832 (which abolished the rotten boroughs sending MPs to Parliament) came an act to abolish them as local oligarchies, and replace them with local councils responsible to their local tax-payers. This was the Municipal Corporations Act of 1835, which led to the creation of the new Newbury Borough Council.

★★

Although the Great Western Railway had opened from London to Bristol in 1841, it did not reach Newbury. It did, however, have a rapid effect on the long-distance traffic carried by the Kennet and Avon Canal. As for the railway, Newbury had to wait for a branch line to be opened from Reading to Hungerford on Tuesday, 21 December 1847, servicing Newbury station. There was no public ceremony to mark the opening, due to illness. To begin with, there were five trains daily along the line in each direction. This line was later extended to Westbury and later still to Penzance. A goods yard was soon added to the east of the station.

Enclosing the open fields

In the Newbury area, many fields were farmed in a traditional style until the late 18th or early 19th century, with the fields divided into strips as they had been in the Middle Ages. Then came the enclosures, which removed the common arable fields and parcelled them up into fenced-off areas, each the private property of its owner. This allowed the adoption of new and improved farming methods, but the less well-off yeoman or commoner frequently suffered in the process.

In the early 19th century, the East and West Fields of Newbury were still divided into strips in the medieval style, although some land had been lost to various enclosures over the centuries. The fields still used a system of crop rotation, a traditional form which had become slightly more sophisticated by the early 19th century. Although they varied, the crops were generally, in year one wheat; in year two barley or oats with or without grass; and in year three clover, peas, beans or fallow. Potatoes and cabbages were also widely grown.

These crops were grown by the owners of the strips or those who leased them, and they were effectively treated as private land until the harvest. Then the rules changed, as they did with most common fields. Newbury residents had the right to turn out their cattle on the fields from the end of the harvest till the 8th of November. They also had a right to take any crops remaining on or in the ground (they could cut any green crops and stubble, and dig up any roots). Some residents gathered sack-loads of potatoes at this time. Neither the owner, nor the person farming the strip had any power to prevent the residents from exercising these rights.

Newbury seen from the south, just below Chandos Road, from a sketch c1840. (West Berkshire Museum).

In the 1840s an attempt was made to enclose part of the land without legal authority, provoking strong opposition. Fences were torn down, trees and shrubs destroyed, and several Newbury residents were sent to jail.

In 1845 came the General Enclosure Act, which meant that each new enclosure did not require a separate Act of Parliament. Newbury Borough applied to the Enclosure Commissioners for a provisional order to enclose the East and West Fields, which was granted in April 1846. The parcels of lands created included a slice through both these fields for the Great Western Railway, allowing it to go ahead with the branch line from Reading (through Newbury) to Hungerford which opened in December 1847. The final Enclosure Award was approved on 31 January 1849, enclosing over 200 acres. Houses were built piecemeal across the newly-enclosed lands as the century progressed, and the different land ownerships are still reflected in the different house-types which can be seen along roads such as Berkeley Road, formerly part of the West Field.

After the East and West Fields came the enclosure of Wash Common, again first proposed by the Borough. A public meeting was held at the Mansion House in January 1855 to discuss who should benefit from the enclosure, and the rights of landholders and Newbury residents. The meeting overwhelmingly backed the motion 'That the enclosure of

Wash Common is expedient in the interests of the town of Newbury', with just three people objecting.

This set the process in motion. Cornelius Davis of East Woodhay was brought in as the surveyor and valuer, to draw up a map showing how Wash Common would be divided, and the enclosure received official approval on 25 February 1858. Historian Walter Money later commented: 'It is scarcely necessary to add that the householders of Newbury received no compensation when thus deprived of the valuable rights and privileges which had been enjoyed by the commonalty of the town for so many centuries …'

★★

The Corn Exchange in the Market Place was designed by J.S. Dodd of Reading and was built 1861–2 as a market for corn, in line with similar buildings at Wallingford and Devizes. It opened on 4 June 1862. Newbury Castle (the symbol of the Borough of Newbury) appears as a relief over the main entrance.

It was effectively a market hall, fairly basic except for the façade, and it remained so for decades. One description of the Corn Exchange shortly before the First World War refers to it still as a large room, covered with advertisements related to corn and agricultural trades. The roof was a single thickness of glass, which gave the farmers and merchants a good light, but there was little or no heating. It had two huge exit doors (in case of fire) and desks scattered about at which the corn dealers sat making their purchases and sales.

The building has been altered and used for a wide range of roles, playing host to a large number of local clubs and societies. It closed in 1988 and was remodelled as an arts centre, re-opening in September 1993.

Several attempts to start newspapers for the Newbury area in the mid-19th century had short-lived success, with the arrival and departure of the *Newbury Telegraph*, the *Newbury Journal* and the *Newbury Advertiser*. Then, in 1867, J. Walter Blacket and Thomas W. Turner started the *Newbury Weekly News*. The first issue went on sale on 7 February, and cost 1½d. In his opening editorial, Turner wrote: 'The *Newbury Weekly News* will aim to represent faithfully the public sentiment of the town and district in which it circulates,' adding, 'The columns of the Newbury Weekly News will be open to correspondence on all questions of general or local importance …'. For many years the paper contained national as well as local news.

The Corn Exchange, seen here in the centre of the picture, was built in 1862 when Newbury was at the centre of an agricultural area.

It was in 1869 that the Borough of Newbury approved proposals to make a new road connecting Cheap Street and Bartholomew Street: the present Market Street. Along with the construction of the new road was to be a new cattle market. This was formally opened by the Earl of Carnarvon in December 1873, with church bells ringing and a banquet for 240 people

The Jubilee Clock in the Broadway, later replaced by the Clock Tower.

at the Mansion House. The market prospered while Newbury remained the heart of a mainly agricultural area, expanding in 1915, but eventually closing in 1969 after some years of decline.

In 1878 the area of Newbury was extended, for the first time incorporating Speenhamland (the whole area around the Clock Tower), and also stretching east to include lands previously in Greenham. The whole area to the north and east of Victoria Park (then still the Marsh), between the River Kennet and the River Lambourn, was also added.

Newbury gained its first elected Member of Parliament in 1885, and the constituency has existed ever since although its boundaries (especially at its eastern end) have changed over time. Before that, the town was represented by the MPs for Berkshire. The first modern MP for Newbury was William George Mount (Conservative), of Wasing Place between Brimpton and Aldermaston.

Newbury Town Hall is a Victorian building in the Market Place, currently home to several organisations including Newbury Town Council. It was built as two separate buildings: one, with a short and a tall tower, fronts the Market Place; the other, which was designed to look like part of the same building, is around the corner and fronts Mansion House Street.

A rare 19th-century view of the Market Place. The Mansion House can just be glimpsed on the right of the picture.

Technically it is the building with the tower, facing the Market Place, which is the Town Hall. This was designed by J.H. Money (Newbury historian Walter Money's brother). Work started in 1878 and the building was completed in 1881; altogether it cost £4,345. The style of the building is said to imitate that of Alfred Waterhouse, who was responsible for the municipal buildings at Reading at around the same time.

The Town Hall has its high clock tower at the corner of the Market Place, with a balcony above the main entrance. Between the two towers, the whole of the first floor is occupied by the Council Chamber, lit by three large windows with stone mullions.

Around the corner, in Mansion House Street, was the Mansion House. This building was demolished in 1908-9, in order to widen Mansion House Street. It was replaced by the narrower 'municipal offices', designed as an extension of the Town Hall.

Newbury Gasworks was established privately in the 1820s, by Joseph Hedley of London, to provide gas mainly for the street lighting associated with the Newbury and Speenhamland Improvement Act. The stone column now at the junction of Speen Lane was erected in October 1828 as a gas light, where the Clock Tower stands now. This 'Speen Obelisk' was provided by Frederick Page of Goldwell House, who became one of those Improvement Commissioners for Speenhamland in July 1825.

Once local government was reorganised in the 1830s, the gasworks was taken over by the new Newbury Borough Council, which ran the premises in Kings Road West (listed at the time variously as Greenham Street, Gashouse Road, Back Lane and Kings Road).

Gas was produced from coal, which was brought in by canal and then by railway after Newbury was connected to the network in 1847. By 1880 the demand for gas at home and work was expanding massively, and the existing gasworks could not supply the necessary pressure. For example, there were problems with the gas lighting at Plenty's Eagle Iron Works, and with the gas engine which drove the machinery of the *Newbury Weekly News*.

The council drew up plans for an extensive new gasworks. This was built beside the railway in King's Road, just west of the junction with Boundary Road, a site which was subsequently occupied by Sterling Cables and later became the Sterling Industrial Estate. It started producing gas in November 1880, and was in full production by the summer of the following year. The new site allowed for expansion, and the amount of gas produced increased rapidly. By 1899 it was producing 33 million cubic feet of gas a year; by 1920, 71 million; by 1930, 118 million.

Residents of Northbrook Street were 'considerably alarmed' in December 1875 by an explosion at the shop of Mr Thomas White, grocer and pork butcher (now Robert Dyas). A gas fitter was testing a pipe, the flame came into contact with the gas, and there was an explosion of great force. A paving stone inside the door was forced up and shattered, the floor was broken into strips and tossed in the air, the windows smashed and the shop's goods thrown about. A bladder of lard was driven upwards with such force that it stuck to the ceiling. Mrs Elizabeth Fennell of the Jack Hotel, who was in the shop at the time, was unhurt but the board on which she was standing was the only sound piece of flooring left on her side of the counter.

Mains water became available in Newbury in 1878, with the opening of the Newbury District Water Works. This included a reservoir at Speen, pumping station at Northcroft, and a well at Northcroft. By 1885 this was supplying water to just over 1,000 houses. The Newbury District Water Company continued to operate the supply until it was acquired by Newbury Borough Council in 1925.

Local schools

The expansion of elementary, or primary, schools in Newbury during the 19th century is complex. A large number of schools were built, and then rebuilt and enlarged, to end the century with systematic provision for the young. The process was driven initially by voluntary contributions, but as the century progressed, the support from taxation (as part of a national system) increased.

In Newbury there were 'National' schools, associated with the Church of England and 'British' schools linked to some of the other Protestant churches. The National schools largely evolved into St Nicolas' School, while the British schools closed and fed their pupils into the Council school established near the railway station.

Newbury had a British school from early in the century (about 1800), in a building at the rear of 81 Bartholomew Street (now the Mango Indian restaurant), and a National school reportedly from 1811. In 1835 an additional National school was built in Speenhamland, which at the time was separate from Newbury. In Newbury, the British boys' school was rebuilt in 1839, with new premises in Newtown Road, at the present St John's roundabout. The British girls' school acquired new premises later, in Station Road. In 1852 Newbury's Wesleyan Methodist church in Northbrook Street, which had previously run just Sunday schools, launched its own Wesleyan day school in buildings behind the church.

The National schools were joined by some charity scholars; in 1827 by pupils of the Kendrick Charity, then by pupils from the Cowslade and Kimber Charities. The schools were in Northcroft Lane, but the premises were inadequate and new purpose-built premises were opened in 1859 in Enborne Road. These housed the National boys' and National girls' schools, which were also known as St Nicolas Schools (in the building with a corner tower, which still survives on the corner of Rockingham Road). The Kendrick's charity pupils were transferred to the British school instead. The National St Nicolas infants' school remained in Northcroft Lane, until moving to West Street in 1872. In 1874 St John's School (also an infants' school) opened in Newtown Road, closely linked to the recently-built St John's church; and St Mary's National infants' school opened in Speenhamland. In 1880 the Speenhamland schools (St Mary's National boys and girls, but not the infants) were enlarged, and they were enlarged again in 1894.

Primary education continued to change and expand, and in 1909 the new Council school opened in Station Road (part of the present

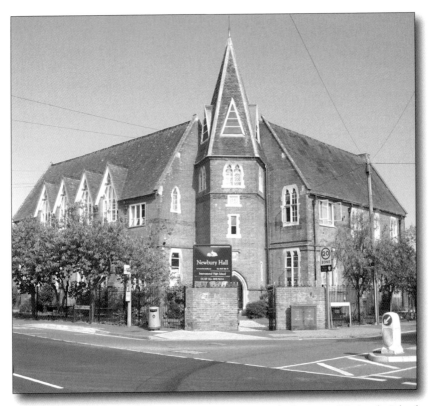

The old St Nicolas' School, Enborne Road, was built as a National School in 1859.

St Nicolas' School site).The Wesleyan day school, and the boys' and girls' British schools all closed, with the pupils transferred to the new Council school.

Although St Bartholomew's School was established in the Tudor period, it was allowed to decline in the late 18th century, with its funds vanishing into the coffers of the unreformed Corporation. It was closed for the early part of the 19th century, and court cases were fought over its future. In 1846 new Trustees agreed to go ahead and revive St Bartholomew's Grammar School. From the income of St Bartholomew's Hospital they were to pay a schoolmaster and an under-master to teach 60 boys, with about 20 free places for boys from Newbury and fee-paying places for 40 others.The boys were to be taught classics, reading, writing, English grammar, mathematics and arithmetic.

The Litten House and School, on the corner of Newtown Road and Pound Street, was rebuilt, with the first stone laid in June 1848. In August 1849 the school reopened with a full complement of boys. The first Master was Henry Newport. The school needed some time to get re-established, but from the 1860s it gained growing success. In 1880 Charity Commissioners gave their backing to the creation of new buildings on fields next to Enborne Road, to provide places for 130 day boys and 20 boarders. A competition for designs received 57 entries, judged by prominent Victorian architect Alfred Waterhouse. The red-brick Tudor-style design of Mr J.H. Porter of London proved the winner, and work started in August 1884. The new school buildings opened on 28 July 1885.

Newbury Hospital

The old Newbury District Hospital on the Andover Road opened in November 1885. Before then, there was a more basic hospital in Pound Street, known as the Navvy Hospital, which was kept busy during the construction of the Didcot, Newbury and Southampton railway. In one incident in 1881 three men were badly injured when their engine left the tracks on the Downs above Compton, and were taken to the Navvy Hospital with heads injuries, a broken thigh and scalding from the boiling water which escaped from the engine.

The expectation that the Navvy Hospital would be closed led to a campaign for a permanent and better hospital, a campaign headed by Dr William T.P. Douglas of Ivy House on the London Road in Newbury. The new hospital was to be financed voluntarily, and Dr Douglas sought support from several wealthy local residents, including Major Thurlow (who was leasing Shaw House), Sir Richard Sutton of Benham Valence, and Mr and Mrs William Chatteris of Sandleford Priory.

A public meeting held at Newbury Town Hall in April 1884, chaired by Lord Carnarvon, heard many arguments in favour of a new hospital. One speaker reported that a man had bled to death while being taken from Burghclere to hospital in Reading. The meeting agreed to establish a Newbury hospital with twelve beds, and subscriptions were invited from the public, raising over £5,000. Work started shortly after the public meeting, and continued until the following year, with Mr H.G. Turner from London as the architect.

The opening day, 18 November 1885, started with a religious service in one of the wards, conducted by the vicar of the nearby St John's church, the Rev. Thomas G. Barlow Poole. Lunch had been prepared in another ward, with champagne to mark the occasion.

When first built, the men's ward had seven beds and the women's ward four. In addition there was a separate one-bed ward, and an operating room which was described at the time as 'exceedingly well lighted and fitted with a hot and cold water service.' There were three bedrooms on the first floor, one for the matron and the others for 'nurses and servants'. The hospital was altered and extended on a number on occasions throughout its 119-year history, until its demolition in 2004, since when it has been replaced by flats for Sovereign Housing.

Beer and Temperance

Many breweries flourished in Newbury in the 19th century, with seven significant businesses operating in the later decades. Working from north to south, at Speenhamland there was Adnams, or the Speenhamland Brewery (just at the beginning of Oxford Street). In Northbrook Street was the Newbury Brewery Company (Somerset's); some of its remaining buildings have recently been demolished to make way for the Park Way development. In Bartholomew Street was the Atlas Brewery, run by Edmund Parfitt, which in 1897 helped to found the South Berks Brewery. Also in Bartholomew Street were Nutley's, later Finn's, which was also known as the Phoenix Brewery; and Westcombe's. In Cheap Street was Flint's, and in West Mills was Hawkins' or the West Mills brewery, which was the other founder of the South Berks Brewery in 1897. The South Berks Brewery then swallowed Flint's Brewery, Westcombe's, J. Platt and Sons of Hungerford, and Blandy and Hawkins of Reading. Writing about the multitude of Newbury's pubs would require a complete history on its own.

The 19th century saw the Temperance Movement become a popular movement in Newbury, campaigning widely against alcohol and encouraging people to abstain. This was reflected in the growth of local Methodist churches, in the creation of coffee houses as an alternative to pubs, to visits and activities organised by a variety of Temperance organisations and even to the establishment of a 'Temperance Hall'. The town itself had a major Methodist church in Northbrook Street, another in Bartholomew Street, chapels at Stroud Green and Wash Common, and numerous other chapels throughout the area. The church in Northbrook Street (originally Wesleyan Methodist), was built in 1837-8, just as Victoria came to the throne. The corner stone was laid on 12 April 1837 by the Rev. Dr Beaumont, and it opened on 16 November 1838. At the time it lay behind other buildings on the street frontage. These were demolished in the late 19th century, opening up the church to public view. The Wesleyan Hall, which used to be at the rear of the church, and was used for Sunday Schools and a variety of meetings, was added in 1887. Another Methodist church (Primitive Methodist) was built on the west side of Bartholomew Street in 1877, along with a minister's house. And a chapel (Primitive Methodist) opened close to Stroud Green in 1874.

The King's Coffee House, in the Broadway, had been established in the 1830s. In 1879 the Newbury Public Coffee House Company was formed, with the specific aim of promoting alternatives to pubs. This company set up the Guildhall Coffee House in Mansion House Street, and the Fountain Coffee House in the City. The movement was strongly supported by those (including the 4th Earl of Carnarvon) urging workers to turn away from pubs and alcoholic drink.

A Temperance Hall was created in Northcroft Lane in 1875, converting a building which had seen a number of uses, including use as the National Schools. It is now better known as the former Arts Workshop, and more recently has housed the Little Bears Day Nursery. On the cornerstone of the building anti-drink slogans can still be seen, spelling out the message, including one which says: 'The drunkard shall come to poverty.' The hall was intended to serve as a base for the large number of national and local Temperance organisations active in the area, many of them associated with the churches. These local organisations included the St Nicolas Church of England Temperance Society (C.E.T.S.); St John the Evangelist C.E.T.S.; St Mary's, Speenhamland C.E.T.S.; Newbury Temperance Band; Independent Order of Good Templars; Independent Order of Rechabites; Stockcross Independent Order of Good Templars; Cold Ash Primitive Methodist; Wickham Heath Primitive Methodist; Shefford C.E.T.S; Shefford Wesleyan and Primitive Methodists; Boxford Wesleyan Methodists; Stroud Green Band; Newbury Primitive Methodist Band of Hope; Stroud Green Primitive Methodist Band of Hope; Wesleyan Band of Hope; Baptist Band of Hope; Congregational Band of Hope; Wash Common Primitive Methodist Band of Hope; Plaistow Green Band; Plaistow Green Primitive Methodist Band of Hope; Brimpton Baptist Band of Hope; Kintbury Wesleyan Methodist; Inkpen Wesleyan Methodist; and Ashmore Green Baptist.

More railways

Two new railways opened in the late 19th century. The first was the Didcot, Newbury and Southampton railway, running north to south

Newbury Temperance Hall, Northcroft Lane was the heart of a thriving movement.

A view of Newbury railway station, c. 1907.

through the whole of the Newbury area. Work started in 1879, and the section between Didcot and Newbury opened in April 1882. In May 1885 the section south from Newbury to Winchester opened. The line arrived into Newbury station from the north-east and Hermitage, cutting under Hambridge Road before curving toward the station. It left heading west with the line towards Hungerford before curving to the south, following the line now used by the A34 Newbury Bypass, to Woodhay and Highclere stations.

In 1898, another branch line opened to the north-west, the Lambourn Valley Railway. This left Newbury station on the west side, on its way to Lambourn. After a few years, West Fields halt was added on the edge of Newbury, becoming the first stop on the line.

Following changes in 1882, Newbury station was altered again in 1900 and then completely rebuilt between 1908 and 1910 as part of the upgrading of the line, which had now become the major rail link to the south-west of England. The result is the vaguely Tudor-style building that stands today.

Chapter 7

The Twentieth Century to 1945

The beginning of the 20th century closely coincided with the end of the Victorian era, which came with Queen Victoria's death in January 1901. In June 1903 a large statue of Queen Victoria was unveiled in the Market Place, presented to the town by the circus showman, 'Lord' George Sanger. He was born in Newbury and said that the place chosen for the statue was the site of the stall his father used to run in Newbury market. The statue was a substantial affair, with a large plinth and four lions, and was created at the Royal Doulton factory in Lambeth. It was removed in March 1933 but parts of it survive, including the statue of Queen Victoria herself which has been in Victoria Park since the 1960s.

Newbury Museum

Newbury Museum opened in 1904, after £2,000 was raised by the people of the town through public subscription. A leading role in the campaign was played by John Rankin, a prominent businessman who ran a drapery shop in Cheap Street and was three times Mayor of Newbury. The 17th-century Cloth Hall just off the Market Place was renovated for the purpose, and opened on 26 October 26 1904. Much of the original collection came from the museum of the Newbury Literary and Scientific Institution, in Northbrook Street.

Harold Peake became involved and was Honorary Curator by July 1909, a position he held until his death in 1946. It was Peake who proposed that the museum's collections should consist of an international section on arts and industries, and a local collection covering the Stone Age to the post-medieval 'modern' period. He saw himself as beginning the task almost single-handed, with difficulties increased by the fact that many of the items in the collection were not labelled. Peake was also

The Cloth Hall which became the home of Newbury Museum (now known as West Berkshire Museum).

involved in practical archaeology, and one of his earliest major projects was a re-excavation of the Anglo-Saxon cemetery discovered at East Shefford in 1889, which took place in 1912. Later excavations included the investigation of Bury's Bank at Greenham.

Peake wrote many books on archaeology and history, including *The Archaeology of Berkshire* (1931), a systematic survey of the available information at that time. He was a member of the national council of the Society of Antiquaries and was President of the Royal Anthropological Institute; and he served for many years as President of the Newbury District Field Club. He lived at Boxford and when he died in 1946, aged 78, his obituary in the *Newbury Weekly News* described him as 'a man of European reputation as an archaeologist, a man whose name was almost a household word among antiquaries of all countries.'

The building which links the Cloth Hall and Granary, extending the museum, was erected in the early 1930s. It was proposed by the Newbury District Field Club, as a memorial to Newbury historian Walter Money. The Club raised a substantial part of the money needed, and it opened in June 1934. The Newbury coat of arms or badge which appears on this part of the museum came from the Queen Victoria statue in the Market Place.

Following the end of Newbury Borough Council and the creation of Newbury District Council, attempts were made to transform what had been largely a Newbury museum (created and supported by the people of the town) into a museum for the whole of the West Berkshire District. It is worth noting that if a Newbury Town Council had been created at that time, the museum could have been transferred to its care, rather than that of the district council. The museum was extended into the Granary, with four new galleries opened in 1984. It was subsequently renamed West Berkshire Museum, and in spite of the new extension its premises were seen as increasingly inadequate for a district-wide role. It ran into difficulties in recent years, and is currently closed pending the outcome of a bid to the Heritage Lottery Fund.

★★

Newbury Free Library opened in 1906, at purpose-built premises in Cheap Street where it remained until the year 2000. A sum of £500 was raised from local people, but the main part of the money came from American steel magnate Andrew Carnegie, a passionate supporter of public libraries, who supplied £2,000. The short road alongside was created at the time, and bears his name. The go-ahead was given by Newbury Borough Council in 1904, and the designs promised an entrance lobby with several newspaper stands, 'so that people in a hurry can get a glance at the news, without entering the building.' It was to have a large reading room, and space for 10,000 books. The foundation stone was laid in 1905, and the first librarian when it opened in May 1906 was Mr J. W. Rosling.

One man was the driving force behind the creation of Newbury Racecourse. This was John Porter, a highly successful racehorse trainer from Park House stables in Kingsclere. The racecourse was a long-standing ambition, and he wanted to site it on land which formed part of the Greenham estate. This was owned by Lloyd Harry Baxendale, chairman of Pickfords for many years. He sold the land needed and supported John Porter in his campaign. Porter approached the Jockey Club for approval, but found his reception like a cold shower. Immediately afterwards, he met King Edward VII, who was a keen racegoer. Porter explained the situation, and the King invited him to discuss his proposal in detail.

With the King's support, Porter gained Jockey Club backing and on 26 April 1904 the Newbury Racecourse Company Limited was created. Porter moved into Newbury, buying a home on Oxford Road which he renamed after one of his winning racehorses – Ormonde House (this was the house which later became the reception building for the old Newbury College, across the roundabout from Waitrose). Contracts agreed in 1904 and 1905 were for £1,500 to build the public stands, and £6,000 to build the stables and neighbouring buildings.

The opening two-day meeting took place in September 1905, when about 15,000 people were present for the first day. The first race was won by *Copper King*, owned by Mr D. J. Pullinger and ridden by Charlie Trigg. The Inaugural Handicap was won by *Missovaja*, owned by Lord Carnarvon from Highclere. The racecourse is still a firm favourite with the Royal family today.

With St Bartholomew's School as Newbury's expanding grammar school but catering just for boys, there was an obvious need for its female equivalent. Newbury Girls Grammar School opened in September 1904 with about 40 girls. It started at the Technical Institute in Northbrook Street, with Miss Esther Luker as the headmistress. She specialised in mathematics, was a keen hockey player, and was to shape the school for almost 30 years. It grew rapidly, in 1910 moving to purpose-built premises on the Andover Road. By 1914 there were 250 girls, and there the school continued until in September 1975 it merged with St Bartholomew's School, becoming co-educational.

*The Queen visiting Newbury racecourse in 2010 (*Newbury Weekly News*)*

Early in the 20th century there were many small courts and passages running off Newbury's main streets, containing a large number of houses and cottages. Normally these houses were rented, and many of them were basically slums. Most of the houses had no toilets, but would share with neighbours, either opposite their front doors or at the end of the yard. Some toilets were missing their doors. Many of these houses had a blank wall at the back, with no back door, and no proper back windows. Water supply in many cases was a tap in the court or passage. And often the court was enclosed with a high wall, which kept out light and did not help with ventilation.

The First World War

For a short period at the beginning of the First World War, Newbury Racecourse was used as a camp for interned aliens and prisoners of war (actually called a 'concentration camp'). Inmates were guarded by the old soldiers of the Berkshire National Reserve, but at the end of 1914 the camp and its guards left the area. At times mounted troops were also based at the racecourse and postcards show their encampment in the centre of the course. Later it was used as a tank repair park, with tanks driven up to Greenham Common for testing. Local people were also employed at the racecourse packing ammunition.

Across the town, many women were employed on war work, and it was women who made large brass shell cases at Plenty's diesel engine works. Production at Elliotts of Newbury included over 200,000 ammunition cases.

The 1914-18 war saw many Newbury men killed; there are 339 names of the First World War dead on the memorial, erected in 1922 outside St Nicolas' church. The names are arranged in deliberately random order, except for the first two: the only woman, Lorna Ferris, who was a nurse in Serbia; and then a man singled out because he was thought to have been the first Newbury man to die, W.J. Himmons. No ranks are included. There are several other memorials in the town, including three inside St Nicolas' church, one in the porch of Newbury post office, and at St Bartholomew's School.

Between the Wars

The range of town centre shops until the middle of the century included several bicycle and motor dealers, mostly family firms, and all of which would carry out repairs. For entertainment, Alphonse Cary in

In 1914 Newbury Racecourse played its part in the war effort by becoming a cavalry camp.

Northbrook Street supplied the needs of those who wanted to make music at home, and even today it is possible to find violins and pianos bearing his name. Povey & Wade, musical instrument dealers, were in Cheap Street. J.J. Davies & Sons were china and glass dealers, founded in 1847 where McDonalds now stands and even mentioned in one of Thomas Hardy's novels. In a section which had been formed from the former carriage entrance, a large grape vine grew.

The local department store, Camp Hopson, opened in Northbrook Street in May 1921, occupying a long range of buildings on the east side of the street – nos. 6 to 14, including everything from today's HSBC to River Island, plus two-thirds of what became Woolworths and is now Wilkinson's. The store was a merger between the Drapery Bazaar, which was established by Alfred Camp in 1886 (and already occupied nos. 6 to 9 Northbrook Street), and the well-established firm of J. Hopson & Sons, on the corner of Northbrook Street and West Street (now partly occupied by Waterstones). This had been founded in the middle of the 19th century by Joseph Hopson. The two companies announced their merger in July 1920; and two months later Hopson heir Paul Hopson married Alfred Camp's daughter, Norah. Of the national chains, Marks & Spencer opened in Newbury in 1935 on a site which was previously occupied by the Jack Hotel. The Jack (which itself was on the site of the largest part

Northbrook Street seen here at the beginning of the 20th century.

of Jack of Newbury's house) closed the previous year and was then demolished. Woolworths arrived in the 1920s and at first sold nothing which cost more than sixpence.

From soon after the First World War, Day Shergold and Herbert held a weekly auction at its sale rooms in Wharf Street (now occupied by the Hogshead pub). This included eggs, poultry, butter, vegetables and other local produce. Buyers came from London and other cities, and in the 1920s more than 30,000 eggs were sold each Thursday. As the century continued the sales changed, eventually falling into a decline. The auction finally closed in 1987.

Well into the century, manufacturing industries were based immediately behind the street frontages, with Plenty's engineering works between Cheap Street and Bartholomew Street, and Elliott's extensive furniture works just behind the Methodist church in Northbrook Street. West Mills and Town Mills were both working watermills, owned by Hovis from 1921.

In 1920 Newbury's first council houses were built, in St George's Avenue. Numbers rose steadily over the decades, with over 1,000 by the mid-1950s and over 2,000 by the early 1970s.

The first cinemas had opened before the First World War. The Newbury Cinema opened in 1910 at the southern end of Cheap Street, thanks to local entrepreneur, Jimmy Tufnail. A month later another was opened, Newbury Picture Palace, immediately south of the Methodist church in Northbrook Street. The building still stands and the slightly overhanging upper floor which housed the projection equipment can still be seen. Grander buildings followed in the 1920s, producing the Regal Cinema in Bartholomew Street (closed 1962); the Central (later Carlton, but better known as the 'flea pit') in Cheap Street, destroyed by fire in 1950; and the Forum in Park Way, which opened in 1939. Newbury had three cinemas when the Second World War broke out, and they continued for the whole of the 1940s. The Forum was the last of these to survive, operating under several names including ABC and Cannon, and finally as a Robins Cinema when it too closed in November 1998.

The Clock Tower in the Broadway was added in 1929, replacing the previous structure (a decorative metal construction generally known as the Jubilee Clock, which had been there since 1889). It was designed by C.R. Rowland Clark, with money donated by Mr J.H. Godding. At the time the name which appeared on the plans was the 'Clock House', and this is how the name has always appeared on official literature produced by those

The Regal Cinema in Bartholomew Street closed in 1962.

from outside the area. For Newbury people, the structure very quickly became known as the 'Clock Tower', and this was the name used in local records within a few years. When the nearby Queen's Arms pub changed its name, adopting that of the nearby structure, it became the 'Clock Tower' pub. Even Hitchman (Newbury) Ltd, the construction company which built it, later claimed 'one of its memorable projects was the construction of the Clock Tower in the Broadway at Newbury'.

Partly in response to the depression of the early 1930s, a local public work programme was started. The 1930s saw the creation of the broad new street Park Way, and improvements to Victoria Park which included the creation of the green and pavilion for Newbury Bowling Club, in the park. More trees were planted and the bandstand was also added at this time.

The Second World War

When the Second World War was declared on 3 September 1939, parts of Newbury Racecourse were immediately requisitioned and a RASC main supply depot set up. However, some racing was able to continue until September 1941. The course was then protected with thick coconut matting and loads of soil and ash, on top of which 37 miles of railway track were laid, along with concrete roads, to form a marshalling yard for the depot supplying the American army (number G 45), which had its headquarters in Thatcham. Petrol was stored there for the landings in North Africa. Later, a wide range of equipment including Bailey bridges and landing mats were gathered there as part of the build-up to the D-Day landings. It was at its peak then, employing nearly 7,000 people and (from July to October 1944) handling supplies which were feeding and clothing 125,000 servicemen a day. Part of the course was used as a prisoner of war camp, and some wall paintings by an Austrian prisoner, Karl Schultz, still survive.

Early in the war the military were concerned about Newbury Bridge as a vulnerable point on the main road from the Midlands to the south coast, and built an additional 'Emergency Bridge' at the end of Park Way, as a wartime measure – a bridge that was to remain largely intact for another 60 years. At the same time, amid fears of invasion, the canal was turned into a defensive barrier across the whole of southern England with the creation of 'pillbox' gun emplacements along its whole length. In addition, many concrete obstacles were prepared – some cylindrical, others cubes or 'dragon's teeth', some of which were set up in Victoria Park.

Many children were evacuated from the London area to Newbury, including two schools. Godolphin and Latymer School, Hammersmith, moved into the Newbury Girls' Grammar School. Both schools shared the premises, with Newbury Girls' having lessons in the mornings and Godolphin in the afternoons. St Gabriel's School moved to Ormonde House in Oxford Road during 1942, and stayed there until it went to Sandleford Priory once the war was over. St Gabriel's, founded in 1929, was run at the time by an order of Anglican nuns called the Companions of Jesus the Good Shepherd.

In terms of its buildings, Newbury did not suffer greatly during the war. Bombs fell on a number of occasions, but mainly did little damage. For example, incendiaries dropped in November 1940 fell on the north porch of St Nicolas' church and caused slight damage to other buildings, while at least eight bombs on two days in March and April 1941 caused no damage. The most serious incident for Newbury occurred on Wednesday, 10 February 1943, when one plane dropped a whole stick of bombs across the town and 15 people died. The bomber was a twin-engined Dornier Do 217. It is still unclear why it bombed Newbury, although the line of approach could suggest that its target was Plenty's Engineering Works (part of the area now occupied by the Kennet Centre). The plane approached Newbury from the south-west, with the first bomb falling south of the St John's crossroads (now a roundabout).

Three women died in Southampton Terrace, Newtown Road. The Victorian St John's church was hit and effectively demolished, but only minor injuries occurred there. Three couples and a woman died at St Bartholomew's Almshouses in Fair Close. At the Council school in Station Road, the caretaker's wife, a carpenter, two teenage girls and a boy died; the headmaster, his wife and an education secretary were badly injured, and several other people had miraculous escapes (the attack happened at about 4.35 pm – if it had taken place earlier, many more would have died at the school). At least one bomb left a crater but caused no real damage, and went unreported at the time. At the Falkland Arms in Market Street a bomb failed to explode.

Shortly afterwards, thirteen of the victims were buried in a communal grave at Shaw cemetery, which was restored in the early 1990s.

Airfields were created in many locations in the Newbury area during the Second World War, including Greenham Common. In May 1941 it became an RAF base and was used for advanced pilot training. The Pearl Harbour attack occurred in December 1941, and the same month

Greenham Common was handed over to the US Army Air Force's 354th Fighter Group, which was equipped with P-51 Mustangs, later replaced by P-47 Thunderbolts.

In 1944, as D-Day approached, the fighters were replaced by C-47 Skytrains and the gliders of the 438th Troop Carrier Group. RAF Greenham Common became the wing headquarters for troop carrier groups based at Welford, Aldermaston, Membury and Ramsbury. All were part of the USAAF's 9th Air Force. On 5 June 1944, on the eve of D-Day, Greenham Common was among the airfields visited by General Dwight D. Eisenhower, Supreme Allied Commander. It was at Greenham that he made a celebrated speech to the paratroopers of the 101st Airborne Division (the 'Screaming Eagles'), saying, 'The eyes of the world are upon you.'

During the war Elliott's of Newbury switched from furniture making to providing parts for aircraft. At first these were made of wood, but as the war progressed the firm extended to the use of aluminium alloy. Output included Horsa gliders, Spitfire components and the fuselages for some de Havilland aircraft. Newbury Diesel Company continued to make ships'

Eisenhower at Greenham Common on the eve of D-Day.

engines. Vickers Armstrong ran a factory at Turnpike, where Spitfire fighter fuselages were made (on the site later occupied by Quantel). Along with other companies, Opperman Gears moved from Islington to Newbury early in the war in order to get out of London, making a wide range of parts including some for Wellington bombers, tanks, and the detection of submarines. Many small engineering firms and even motor garages were used to make aircraft parts.

Many people played active parts in the war, in military and civil roles, and it is probably wrong to single anyone out. However, the name of Ron Lambert will be widely known, as for a long time afterwards he photographed local events for the *Newbury Weekly News*. He went through the North Africa campaign with the Army Photographic Unit, and then through the Italian campaign. His stories included being blown off an Italian quayside by a bomb blast, and helping to take the surrender of an Italian village when he found himself ahead of the front line. His photographs of both campaigns are in the Imperial War Museum.

In 1945, as the war drew towards its end the 'Dig for Victory' campaign finished and, in April, Newbury Borough Council dissolved its 'Emergency Committee', which had been responsible for the town during wartime. In May, Civil Defence organisations were wound up. By July, arrangements were being made to switch the street-lighting back on, and to replace road-signs which had been removed 'for the duration'. Many clubs and societies were revived, including Newbury Cricket Club which started to prepare its Northcroft pitch ready for use for the 1946 season. Some services were reduced or closed, like the British Restaurant. This had started in 1940 at the Council school as a 'Communal Kitchen' mainly for evacuees. By 1943 when it was renamed the British Restaurant, it was open to all and regularly serving over 400 main meals a day, at less than a shilling each, with regular customers including people from the nearby almshouses. It closed in 1947. Other services continued. The nursery school in Victoria Park had started in August 1942, mainly to release mothers for war work. It continued with short-term leases and in temporary buildings, until a new school was built over 40 years later.

On the War Memorial there are 171 names of Newbury people who died in the Second World War. They appear arranged in alphabetical order, except for several names added at the end, which include those of the fifteen who died in the bombing of Newbury in 1943.

Chapter 8

Newbury since 1945

Newbury College has grown steadily since the 1940s. It evolved out of the Technical Institute at 60 Northbrook Street, and opened in Oxford Road in 1948 (originally as the Newbury Institute of Further Education). The college took over Ormonde House, which had been vacated by St Gabriel's School. For the first few years the Principal lived on the top floor, and buildings in the grounds included the affectionately-named 'chicken shed'. When it started, there were just four full-time members of staff. In the autumn term of 1948 there were 1,000 students for 50 classes, and 71 evenings classes attracted a further 1,350 students. It expanded steadily, and several building programmes followed, changing the face of the college. For many years it was the South Berks College of Further Education, and in 1975 it changed its name to Newbury College.

After several decades at Oxford Road the college moved to a new site on the opposite side of Newbury, off Monks Lane. The new multi-million pound complex was built as part of the Private Finance Initiative (PFI), with the contract signed in 2001. The move took place over the summer of the following year, with the college opening at its new campus premises in September 2002. Later the same year work started on the demolition of the old college buildings, including Ormonde House, and their replacement by housing.

New facilities for the elderly were built at Fair Close, partly on the site of the St Bartholomew's Almshouses which had been destroyed by the bombing in 1943. The development included blocks of flats to the side and rear, as well as the day centre itself which was opened by the Queen Mother in 1967.

Some surprisingly well-known 1960s groups played Newbury, including the Who, Jimi Hendrix and Cream. The two main venues were the Plaza and the Corn Exchange, both in the Market Place. For example, at the Corn Exchange in 1966 were the Who, described as 'chartsmashing'

Ormonde House, home of the man who started Newbury Racecourse, and for many years used as the reception for Newbury College before it moved to its present site in Monks Lane.

(May); Georgie Fame and the Blue Flames (June); the Yardbirds (June); and Geno Washington and the Ram Jam Band (August).

At the Plaza in 1966 were the Pretty Things (March); the Merseys, formerly the Merseybeats (March and June); Cliff Bennett and the Rebel Rousers (May); MI5 (May); Johnny Kidd and the Pirates (June); Billy J. Kramer and the Dakotas (September); Geno Washington (December, then returning several times). In 1967 bands included the Jimi Hendrix Experience (February); Cream (April); and John Mayall's Blues Breakers (May).

Until the 1960s, the A34 ran down Newtown Road and Bartholomew Street, crossing the 18th-century Newbury Bridge into Northbrook Street, up to the Clock Tower and continued along Oxford Street and Oxford Road. The problems were obvious, and Newbury was one of the towns included in the Buchanan Report of 1963, *Traffic in Towns*, which aimed to explore different approaches to dealing with traffic.

Western Avenue was built to take A4 through-traffic away from the Clock Tower area; and the 'north-south relief road' (known as the 'ring road') was constructed to take through traffic out of the town centre. This dual-carriageway included new bridges across the railway and the Kennet.

After several delays, the section south from the Kings Road (police station) roundabout to the Queens Road (Gowrings) roundabout eventually opened in February 1965. The section linking the King's Road roundabout with London Road (Robin Hood) opened that September.

The relief road avoided Newbury town centre, but through traffic was still using Newtown Road and Oxford Road. Several years after the M4 opened in 1971, the Donnington Link was built to replace the old Oxford Road and provide better access to the motorway. In 1979 the Sandleford Link opened to take traffic directly south from the Gowrings (now Burger King) roundabout to Pinchington Lane.

These steps created a new north-south route for through traffic, which grew in volume. Expanding car ownership and development in the area also contributed to a growth in traffic, and by the 1980s the new 'relief road' was regularly congested between the Robin Hood and Gowrings roundabouts.

Newbury Cattle Market closed in 1969, a significant change which was seen by many as symbolising the end of Newbury's centuries-old role as an agricultural market town. The cattle market had flourished in the early

Closing the cattle market signified the end of Newbury as an agricultural market town. This photograph dates from 1924 and shows Mr Arthur T. Watson, the auctioneer, with gavel raised. (Dreweatts 1759, Newbury)

20th century, but increasingly farmers sold directly to dealers and as a result, it was generally the smaller farmers who frequented the market. The fall in numbers was pronounced in the 1950s and 1960s. The end came in June 1969 and for the last sale, Mr Desmond Barton sold a calf to Mr Philip Povey of Kingsclere for £10 2s 6d. A multi-storey car park was built on a large part of the site.

The Kennet Centre

In the 1960s work started on the Kennet Centre, a shopping centre in the heart of Newbury. The site is a triangle bounded by Cheap Street, Market Street and Bartholomew Street, and much of it had been occupied by the engineering firm Plenty, which moved out to Hambridge Road in 1965. The first phase ('The Mall'), which opened in 1972, saw Sainsbury's supermarket as the main store and 21 other shops, some around an open square and others (including the Gas showroom) fronting Cheap Street. Phase II involved stretching this to the north, with a new covered lane of shops which opened in 1985.

Not everyone was happy with the change. As Newbury librarian Helen Purvis wrote: 'Under the bulldozer went wattle and daub walls, Tudor gables, and historical associations; the house in which Lord Falkland received his last communion before the First Battle of Newbury; [and] the old King's Head, once the premises of a maker of strings for the longbow in the 15th century.'

At this time a multi-storey car park occupied the south side of Market Street, and the bus station was close to the corner of Market Street and Bartholomew Street. Phase III of the Kennet Centre involved extending Sainsbury's into part of the bus station site, and building a department store stretching from the existing parts of the centre through to Bartholomew Street (Debenhams). However, it was Sainsbury's which was ultimately responsible for switching the multi-storey and the bus station to opposite sides of Market Street, demolishing the old concrete multi-storey and replacing it with a car park in brick. In spite of this, in 1994 Sainsbury's dealt the Kennet Centre a blow when it moved out to a new site in King's Road, next to the ring road. Its Kennet Centre shop was sub-divided, and the centre lost its anchor store. Finally, after a strong public campaign, a cinema was built over the surface car park at the corner of Cheap Street and Market Street, with shops underneath, opening in November 2009.

★★

The M4 motorway opened through the Newbury area on 22 December 1971, making the area far more accessible for business and commuters. A 50-mile length from Swindon to Maidenhead opened that day, the last stretch of the M4, completing the motorway from London to Cardiff. Over 100 cars queued in the rain to get onto the motorway at Chieveley as soon as it had opened, and bridges across the new road were lined by people waving to the motorists below. Before the motorway, much of the traffic travelling towards London from Newbury would have to take the A4, and travel through Reading. It became feasible for commuters to work in or close to London while living in Newbury.

The amount of housing in Newbury expanded steadily during the 20th century, although its counterpart was the demolition of the courtyards off Newbury's main streets, generally categorised as slum or sub-standard housing. The whole Wendan Road/Chandos Road area was built up, with much of the housing associated with the expansion in employment which accompanied the creation of the Atomic Weapons Research Establishment (AWRE, now AWE) at Aldermaston, and AERE at Harwell; as was much housing in the Elizabeth Avenue/Valley Road area. An extensive estate was built from the 1950s in the Kiln Road and Turnpike Road area. Other developments included the Nightingales estate which received the go-ahead in 1968. Also in the late 1960s, approval was given for the development of Wash Common as housing. Much of the residential development in and around the town in the 1970s and 1980s was associated with the developers Trencherwood, established by John Norgate in 1972. Following the death of John Norgate, Trencherwood was taken over by David Wilson Homes. The new housing is pushing the built-up area of Newbury in all directions, and it is David Wilson Homes which is developing the current scheme to build 1,500 houses and flats on part of the Newbury Racecourse site, in Greenham, along with other changes.

In 1972 the Local Government Act was passed, in an attempt to provide a clearer structure for council services. This changed the shape of Berkshire, with the northern part, including Abingdon and the Vale of the White Horse, becoming part of Oxfordshire. The Newbury area up until then was often referred to as South Berkshire. The 1972 Act abolished Newbury Borough Council and Newbury Rural District Council. They were replaced by Newbury District Council (covering the whole of West Berkshire), which was formed in 1973 and took over in 1974.

In Newbury itself, there was an option to create a town council (basically a form of parish council) but this was rejected at the time, and

In October 1996 The Queen paid a visit to Newbury, marking the 400th anniversary of the granting of the town's Royal Charter. She is seen here in the Town Hall talking with Donald Willis, then Chairman of the Newbury Weekly News. *(Newbury Weekly News)*

instead a body was created for Newbury which was mainly ceremonial, called the Charter Trustees. This ensured that Newbury continued to have a mayor, but meant that much of the Borough Council's property and the services it had built up over the years were transferred to the District Council. These included Newbury Museum, the Corn Exchange and Victoria Park.

Eventually, Newbury Town Council was created in 1997 as a replacement for the Charter Trustees. Some powers were transferred from Newbury District Council, where decisions affecting Newbury had been taken by councillors from across the whole of West Berkshire. The first elections to the new Town Council were in May 1997.

More changes came in 1998, when Berkshire County Council (the 'Royal County of Berkshire') was abolished and its responsibilities (including those for schools and old peoples' homes) transferred to several unitary authorities. It was at this time, with its change in status, that Newbury District Council became West Berkshire Council.

Restoring the canal

By the end of the Second World War, the Kennet and Avon Canal had spent nearly a century in the ownership of the Great Western Railway, and had gone into a stately decline. It was not a high priority for politicians when the railways were nationalised. But it was the British Transport Commission (BTC), which became responsible for the canal in February 1949, that decided that it had no future.

In the meantime, a movement for supporting Britain's inland waterways was just emerging, with the Inland Waterways Association (IWA) formed in 1946. Newbury resident John Gould wrote to the *Newbury Weekly News* urging that the canal should be kept open, and public meetings discussed the future of the canal, winning new supporters. Early in 1948 the Kennet and Avon branch of the Inland Waterways Association was formed, with John Gould as secretary.

There was an attempt to revive commercial traffic on the canal, with John Knill and John Gould taking cargoes such as grain and salt. But in June 1950, the BTC closed a stretch of the canal between Heales Lock (just west of Woolhampton) and Burghfield Lock, stopping access to the Thames at Reading. The Newbury canal supporters now had a fight on their hands, and wanted to devote their efforts to the Kennet and Avon rather than canals as a whole. In August 1951 Newbury broke away from the IWA and formed the Kennet and Avon Canal Association. The canal continued to deteriorate. In April 1952 Higgs Lock, west of Newbury, became unusable.

John Gould initiated a widely-supported High Court action against BTC on the grounds that they had failed in their legal duty to keep the canal navigable. It was heard in July 1955, and (according to *The Times*) the judge Mr Justice Roxburgh referred to Higgs Lock and stated in a reserved judgement: 'The defendants well knew ... that their failure to repair it was unlawful, but they hoped, he supposed, that no bargee would be able to find the means to contest their inaction in the High Court ...', adding, 'If that was the law, then it was the duty of a statutory monopoly to obey it, just as much as anyone else.' John Gould was awarded £5,000, but he failed in a bid for an injunction preventing BTC from causing the deterioration of more of the canal.

However, as a result of the case BTC admitted that they intended to close the canal, and were introducing a Bill to achieve this. Already there were branches of the Kennet and Avon Canal Association at Devizes (1952), the Vale of Pewsey (1952), Bath (1954) and Reading (1955). Together they ran a campaign against the Bill, with 20,000 signatures collected on a petition against closing the canal. The petition was carried from Bristol to London along the canal (passing through Newbury on 19 January 1956) before being presented to Parliament. The campaign did not stop the Bill being approved, in that the BTC won the legal right not to restore navigation along the whole canal. However the campaign against the Bill, which included local authorities and many individuals, succeeded in adding an amendment which required enough maintenance in the short term to ensure there was no further deterioration. This effectively protected the canal until the BTC was replaced by the British Waterways Board, four years later. The reorganisation provided the real prospect of restoring the whole canal, even though most of the money would have to be raised from voluntary contributions. It was this change in approach which led to the change in name, with the Kennet and Avon Canal Trust incorporated on 6 June 1962 to take over from the Association, raising money and co-ordinating a volunteer effort which contributed massively to the restoration of the canal, stage by stage.

Work began in 1965 on Sulhamstead Lock towards Reading, which cost £7,000 (all raised by voluntary contributions) and reopened in 1968. Three locks between Hamstead and Kintbury were reopened in May 1972 (opening the waterway from Newbury to Kintbury), and the canal reopened to Hungerford in 1974. Work continued between Newbury and Reading, with Tyle Mill and Towney locks reopening in 1976. By 1979 it was possible to cruise from Newbury west to Little Bedwyn.

The process of restoration continued until by 1988 only two gaps remained: the Caen Hill flight of locks at Devizes; and two locks and three swing bridges which needed to be rebuilt at the Newbury end.

The whole canal was officially reopened by the Queen at Devizes in 1990, although restoration continued afterwards as more work and money were required. By 1990, it seemed clear that the canal had been saved for the future. For his efforts in support of the Kennet and Avon Canal over decades, John Gould was appointed MBE in 1992. He died in 1999, and even his funeral procession was along the canal. His bust can be seen upstairs in Newbury Library, looking towards the Wharf.

Greenham Common

In 1979, during the Cold War, it was announced that American Cruise missiles would be based in the UK. They would carry nuclear warheads. The following June, Defence Secretary Francis Pym said that Greenham Common was one of the two UK bases which would be used. Six flights of Tomahawk Cruise missiles would be stationed there. The theory was that at a moment of crisis these would be driven off the base in their purpose-built transporters, to scatter before the missiles were launched. From the moment of the announcement, Greenham became the subject of international news and controversy.

Six thick-walled concrete silos were built to the south-west of the runway. In July 1982 the (USAF) 501st Tactical Missile Wing was officially activated at RAF Greenham Common and in November 1983 the first Cruise missiles arrived.

In view of the controversy they caused, it is surprising (on looking back) to realise that it was only just over five years after the missiles arrived that the Intermediate-Range Nuclear Forces (INF) treaty was signed by the US and Russian leaders, Ronald Reagan and Mikhail Gorbachev, agreeing to their removal.

In March 1991 the last of the Cruise missiles were flown out, and in June the USAF base was officially 'inactivated', and the 501st Tactical Missile Wing stood down. However, it was not until September 1992 that the final withdrawal of the USAF from Greenham took place.

The Greenham Peace Camp began in 1981, between the announcement of Greenham Common as a missile site and their arrival. It started almost accidentally. In August 1981 a group set out to walk from Cardiff to Greenham, as a non-violent protest against nuclear weapons. This was the 'Women for Life on Earth' march, which reached Greenham early in September. News coverage had been poor and so, with inspiration from the suffragettes, four women chained themselves to the fence near the

The first Greenham women at the fence in 1981. (Keith Pritchard)

main gate. That evening a camp-fire was lit, in the following days supporters brought in food and other supplies, and the Peace Camp was established (at the main gate on the A339, or 'yellow gate.'). Action on a small and large scale followed, with one of the first being an attempt in December to stop sewerage pipes being laid. Although the march and the camp had consisted mainly of women from the beginning, it was not until February 1982 that the decision was made to make it a women-only camp.

From May 1982 there were regular attempts to evict the women. Protest grew as the missile silos were built, with three more camps established and, on New Year's Day in 1983, women climbed the fence to dance on the (empty) silos. A new camp was established near the silo entrance ('green gate'), and in April the women joined CND in a mass demonstration with the aim of forming a human chain to link Greenham with Aldermaston and Burghfield. Some figures put the number who took part at 70,000. In July 1983 'blue gate' was established (at the top of Pyle Hill) and 'orange gate'. Another four camps at four more gates were set up in December 1983, immediately after the arrival of the missiles. The same month came another demonstration, the 'Refuse Cruise' weekend, also called 'Reclaim the Common'. Up to 50,000 took part, according to the organisers.

Protest died down after 1987, but the camps stayed. After the last of the Cruise missiles left Greenham, the camp at Pyle Hill continued until January 1994, while the camp at the main gate carried on until September 2000, nineteen years after it was first established.

Newbury's reaction to the women and the camps was sharply divided. There were many strong supporters, offering the use of their homes, and supplying food, fuel and other needs, as well as taking part in the demonstrations or actions. Opposition varied from political disagreement, to local shops barring the women, and to the establishment of an anti-peace women group, Residents Against Greenham Encampments (RAGE), which took out a series of advertisements against the women in the local press in 1984.

From the moment the decision to remove the missiles was announced there had been heated discussion about the future of Greenham. Many wanted the whole of Greenham Common to be returned to common land. The USAF finally withdrew in September 1992, and the following year the Ministry of Defence put the common up for sale. The runways were demolished, with much of the rubble being used in the construction of the Newbury Bypass. There was considerable negotiation, but the outcome was that in March 1997, Greenham Common (the whole base) was bought by the Greenham Common Trust for £7 million. The Trust had been specially set up for this purpose, and the same day sold the open common (all except the built-up area to the south of the runway) to Newbury District Council for a symbolic £1. The leading role in establishing the Trust (which had Newbury District Council as a 20% stakeholder) was taken by Sir Peter Michael. The Trust kept the built-up area to rent out for commercial purposes as New Greenham Park; however, income from the rental would go to local causes.

In April 2000, the public was once again given access to Greenham Common after removal of the fence (although the area round the silos remained fenced-off). Two years later the future of the common was safeguarded with the Greenham and Crookham Commons Act 2002, which recognised the majority of Greenham Common as common land.

★★

Shopping in Newbury and elsewhere has changed dramatically since the war, and food shopping illustrates this clearly. The town was previously well served by grocers and 'provision merchants', many of them local businesses, including well-known names such as Kimbers on the corner of Bartholomew Street and Pound Street. But chain stores were already well represented by names such as International Stores (Bartholomew Street), Baylis (Northbrook Street), David Greig (Northbrook Street) and the Co-op (Cheap Street). It was the chains which led to moves towards self-service supermarkets in the late 1950s and early 1960s, adding shops such as Liptons (first in Bartholomew Street, then Northbrook Street). Steadily the size of the supermarkets and the number of checkouts increased, with Tesco arriving in Northbrook Street in the late 1960s, and Sainsbury in 1972.

Sainsbury's store opened as one of the original occupants in the Kennet Centre development. It was considerably enlarged in the 1980s, and in 1994 moved out to a larger site off Kings Road. This store was then expanded in turn, putting an upper deck onto the car park in order to free up land. The store also had a first floor added, with the whole redevelopment completed in August 1999.

A Tesco supermarket opened in Northbrook Street in the late 1960s (in the building currently occupied by HMV), and continued there in the 1970s and 1980s. With the move towards larger supermarkets, Tesco then acquired a site on Pinchington Lane to build a new superstore, and the town centre supermarket closed. The superstore proved a great commercial success, and was expanded on the same site, branded as a 'Tesco Extra'. In the mid-1990s a smaller Tesco supermarket was opened in Northbrook Street, in the building which had been occupied previously by David Greig, Key Markets and Gateway, this time branded as a 'Tesco Metro'. And in May 2010 a third Tesco was opened on London Road.

Waitrose has had a Thatcham store for a number of years, but more recently opened in Newbury on the old Southern Electricity site off Oxford Road.

The evolution of shopping in this way has seen the closure not only of smaller grocers, but of many specialist shops such as greengrocers, butchers and even fishmongers and newsagents, and the concentration of shoppers in the larger stores now represented in Newbury by Tesco, Sainsbury and Waitrose.

Newbury came off relatively lightly in the Great Storm of October 1987, although many trees came down, roads were blocked, and 60,000 homes in the surrounding area were left without electricity, some of them for up to a week. Houses lost slates and tiles, while among the fallen trees were many along the banks of the Kennet and Avon Canal, including a massive horse chestnut in Victoria Park. The wind speed locally had reached 80 mph.

The town was badly hit by a storm in 1990, when high winds led to many trees being blown down or uprooted in January. High-sided vehicles were overturned on the M4, and a van driver died on the A34 at Newtown. There was extensive damage to property: The roof was peeled off at John Rankin junior school, temporary classrooms at Greenham Court School (now The Willows) were demolished, and again many houses lost slates and tiles. Thousands were left without power or communications as poles carrying electricity and telephone cables were brought down, and there was localised flooding.

The Newbury Bypass

The idea of a Newbury bypass, taking the north-south road, the A34, around the town, had been talked about for decades before it was opened in 1998. In 1963 the Buchanan Report had assumed that Newbury would receive an A34 bypass to the west of Newbury, and explored other changes to local roads on that basis.

Preparations for the bypass began after the completion of the M4, with the Department of Transport starting work on a scheme in 1976. In 1982 there was large-scale consultation on alternative routes. The main alternatives were an eastern route, which ran into difficulties because it had to cope with the then-active RAF Greenham Common (going round the runway), and with Newbury Racecourse; a central route, in the form of a flyover directly above the 'ring road' dual carriageway (then the A34, later – after the bypass was built – renumbered A339); and a western route, running mainly through open countryside. There were several variations on these three themes. In 1984 the Department of Transport announced that it favoured a western route, and shortly afterwards the cost was estimated at £25 million. Public enquiries followed in 1988 and 1992, confirming the route, and construction tenders were invited in 1994.

Strong arguments were ranged on both sides of the debate about the road. Locally, SPEWBY (the Society for the Prevention of the Western Bypass) had been formed in 1982 to oppose the western bypass, and there was also a Newbury Bypass Supporters' Association. The arguments against tended to be environmental and ecological; the main arguments in favour focused on local traffic problems in and around Newbury, although for the Department of Transport the over-riding issue was reducing delays for long-distance traffic.

The campaign against the bypass got into gear in 1995, with hundreds attending a Friends of the Earth rally at Donnington Castle in July. The peak of opposition came in the first three months of 1996, when protestors attempted to stop work on clearing the route of the bypass. This was flagged up well in advance, with the national press producing headlines such as 'Anti-road army digs in for battle of Newbury'. A lot of attention was given to complex tunnels built by the protestors. In spite of the publicity, the protestors gained initial successes, when a manned tripod erected in the road effectively blockaded the Sulhamstead farm being used as a base by the security guards. On 10 January demonstrators clashed with security guards after ten trees were felled at Great Pen Wood. Eight security guards and a protestor were treated in hospital.

In February 1996 the Newbury bypass was the focus for the largest anti-road demonstration in British history. Six thousand people walked through Snelsmore Common to attend a rally at Bagnor. Protestors had set up camps at Snelsmore, Bagnor, Elmore, Kennet, Redding's Copse, and The Chase, but at the end of February 1996 they lost their legal battle against eviction. The sequence of evictions began straight away, and one of the memorable images was the use of specialised climbers to remove protestors who had established themselves in trees in order to prevent them being cut down.

By early April 1996, the route had been cleared. Over 1996 as a whole, more than 1,000 arrests were made, mainly for public order offences and obstruction.

Swampy and Co., protestors against the Newbury bypass, took to the trees in 1996.
(Newbury Weekly News)

The contract for building the bypass was awarded to Costain Civil Engineering for £73.7 million, and work started once the route was cleared. The contract was for 13.5 kilometres (8.5 miles) of dual carriageway, which included 30 bridges/ underpasses required to take the bypass over or under existing roads and footpaths. There were complex junctions north of Newbury (the 'Donnington Link interchange'), with the A4, on the Andover Road and at Tot Hill. A long section at the southern end followed the route of the old Didcot, Newbury and Southampton railway. The centre section included an embankment across the Kennet Valley, which used thousands of tons of crushed hardcore from the demolition of the long runway at nearby Greenham Common. Protest did not stop, but it lost much of its edge once it was clear that the road was under construction. In January 1997 there was an anti-bypass rally at Speen and Stockcross.

The Newbury bypass opened quietly at 1.20 am on Tuesday, 17 November 1998. The first car was a Volkswagen Golf led along the bypass by two police patrol cars. Nine hours later, the bypass was officially opened by the chief executive of the Highways Agency, Lawrie Haynes. The final cost, including policing, was over £100 million, more than four times the cost suggested in the 1980s.

Those who benefited most were drivers of through traffic, avoiding the delay on the Newbury roundabouts, and developers who are still in the process of adding residential development to Newbury, with the consequence that traffic on the ring road is returning to pre-bypass levels.

Industry in Newbury

During the 20th century Elliotts of Newbury manufactured a range of furniture, including bedroom and dining suites, at their premises behind the Methodist church. After the war, in 1945, they were not at first allowed to return to furniture manufacture, so they made a series of sports gliders including the *Olympia*, many of them for export. For a long time the company was Newbury's largest employer: There were over 500 on the payroll in 1965, though this number rapidly decreased. In December 1974 came the surprise announcement that the firm was to close, a process completed by the following Easter.

After the war, Plenty Ltd continued in the Eagle Iron Works between Cheap Street and Bartholomew Street. In 1965 it moved to purpose-built premises on a 19-acre site in Hambridge Road, producing a range of pumps, filters and mixers, primarily for the oil industry. In the 1970s over three-quarters of its products were exported, with the Middle East as a major customer. The expansion of the North Sea oilfields also provided a major opportunity. It was acquired by the SPX Corporation in 2001, and its name has changed to SPX although the Plenty name is retained for some of its products.

Opperman Gears continued at its Hambridge Road site after the war, becoming Opperman Mastergear and making industrial power transmission products and gearboxes for the valve industry. Much of its site has now been cleared to provide an access for the planned development at Newbury Racecourse, but it still retains a presence in Hambridge Lane.

Newbury has provided a home for a number of state-of-the-art computer companies, helping to make the Thames Valley or M4 corridor something of a UK 'Silicon Valley'.

Quantel started life as part of (Sir) Peter Michael's Micro Consultants at West Mills in 1969. It became a separate company in 1973 and moved to Turnpike Road, where it has remained ever since. The firm developed the conversion of images to a digital state and then led the world in the manipulation of television images and film editing, with the development of equipment such as the Paintbox and Harry. The company was acquired by UEI and then Carlton Communications, and had over 400 employees in the 1990s. In 2000 it regained independence following a management buy-out.

Micro Focus was founded in 1976 to design, develop and market business applications for computers. Its fortunes dipped in the mid-1980s, rose, and then dipped again in the early 1990s. It has occupied several premises in the town, but the Newbury office has been based in a modern extension at The Lawn since a radical reorganisation in 1996.

Greenham Business Park was created in 1997 as New Greenham Park. When Greenham Common was bought by Greenham Common Trust in March 1997, the Trust acquired the built-up area near the main gate which had been used for aircraft hangars and a range of other facilities. This was transformed by the Trust into an industrial/commercial area, then called New Greenham Park. Properties here were leased to businesses, and the income became the revenue for the Greenham Common Trust. A large proportion of the rents generated are used to aid local community projects. This was £100,000 in 2001, and by 2011 the Trust declared that it had given £15 million to local charities. The name of New Greenham Park was changed in 2011 to Greenham Business Park and it currently hosts over 100 businesses, employing about 1,500 people; while further areas are 'under development'.

Other major local companies include Bayer and Stryker. Bayer plc, the international pharmaceutical and chemical company, moved its UK and Ireland headquarters from Surrey to new offices on the site of the former Elliott's factory, with the address as Strawberry Hill. The extensive complex was officially opened in April 1984 by the chairman of Bayer AG, the German parent company.

Stryker makes and supplies joint replacements and a range of other items in the medical devices or orthopaedic market. It has been based in Canal View Road, off Hambridge Road, and this summer (2011) saw the completion of its £15 million UK headquarters on the opposite side of Hambridge Road.

Mobile phone and telecommunications company Vodafone emerged in the mid-1980s, and steadily expanded for fifteen years before building its global headquarters on an open field at the entrance to the town. It was

The Newbury Agricultural Show seen here in 1981, at Shaw, on what is now the Vodafone headquarters. Three years later the showground moved to its present site at Chieveley and is now known as the Royal County of Berkshire Show.

Vodafone's new headquarters was given the go-ahead in 1999. (By kind permission of Vodafone)

set up in April 1985 as a subsidiary of Racal, first called Racal Telecom. Gerald Whent was its chief executive until 1996, with Ernest Harrison as chairman. In its early years, when BT was its only competitor, Racal Telecom took more than half of the British mobile phone market

It was floated on the stock exchange in 1989, and two years later as a fully independent company, changed its name to Vodafone. As mobile phone ownership grew, Vodafone gradually acquired more and more premises in Newbury until it had just over 50 separate offices, dominating employment in the town. Many a delivery driver heading for Newbury had a small moment thinking how easy it had been finding the Vodafone address, before trying to establish which building was the right target.

Vodafone put forward plans for purpose-built headquarters on the former Newbury Showground at Shaw, next to the A339 north of Newbury. This was on an open field owned by former county councillor Genevieve Fairhurst which had not been earmarked for development and there was strong local opposition to the proposal. Green campaigners feared it would lead to further development of green-belt land. Vodafone argued that if the council did not approve the development, it would be forced to leave Newbury. Its employees marched in support of the plans which were narrowly approved by West Berkshire Council in April 1999.

By February 2000 Vodafone had grown strong enough to pull off a £100 billion hostile takeover of German telecommunications firm Mannesmann. In May the same year, work started on its new headquarters at Shaw. The first staff moved in during August 2002.

★★

A new Newbury library opened on Newbury Wharf in July 2000, replacing the building in Carnegie Road.

A new hospital for the Newbury area was built between the London Road and Turnpike Road, between Newbury and Thatcham, known as West Berkshire Community Hospital, opening in March 2004. The old Newbury and Sandleford hospitals were demolished, and their sites sold as part of the redevelopment. This hospital provides a range of services

The new hospital – West Berkshire Community Hospital.

locally, using local GPs and visiting specialists, but the nearest Casualty departments remain at Reading and Basingstoke.

Parkway in Park Way

Newbury town centre changed significantly from the 1960s, with the construction of the Kennet Centre and the closure of the cattle market. But in 2005 came plans for the biggest change so far, the construction of a large shopping centre between Northbrook Street and Park Way, from Park Street to Marsh Lane and beyond.

Park Way had, since the 1930s, provided a large and easily accessible surface car park, and there were additional well-used car parks behind Marks & Spencer and behind no. 31 (for many years Swifts' Cleaners), all owned by West Berkshire Council. However, the general appearance of the area was run-down, and in particular this was the case for the buildings which had formerly been part of or adjacent to Newbury Brewery's premises (behind nos. 25-29). These included Sunstore, which burnt down, and a building which was Humphries Exhaust Centre for many years before becoming a car wash. A gym and a hairdresser were among other occupants in this area.

The new Parkway Shopping Centre seen from Victoria Park.

The planning applications put forward in 2005 by Standard Life Investments involved building a two-storey 550-space underground car park across a large part of the site, filling the whole area with shops, and creating a new street between Northbrook Street and Park Way, and parallel to both. Another new street would connect with Northbrook Street opposite West Street, with the name East Street. Argos' premises in Northbrook Street were demolished to create the junction, along with the adjacent Automagic/ Timpsons. Flats would be built on top of the shops, with a tower facing Victoria Park. Originally the development included an open square at its southern end, but as the development evolved this was replaced by a plan for a 'John Lewis at Home' store. As finalised, the development includes more than 300,000 square feet of shops, and 147 new flats.

A number of listed buildings were demolished to make way for the development, including the early 19th century building housing Argos and listed former brewery buildings in the area behind Uncle Henry's/the Castle pub, such as a building on Marsh Lane described as a former malthouse. Although these were of interest to industrial archaeologists, they had been shabby for years and many Newbury people were not sad to see the end of them.

More important was a generally unknown old building up towards Park Street, behind no. 45 Northbrook Street (Casino Slots) in an alley known as Caroline Place. Here the plans proposed total demolition of the building, on the north side of the alley. Part of this building was identified as 16th-century, with other Tudor timber-work included in the rest of the building. It had been altered, but was described as 'of interest as a surviving fragment of a post-medieval range extending behind a listed building.' In spite of the attention drawn to this building, West Berkshire Council approved demolition.

The Parkway development opened in late 2011. The council and developers' declared aim for Parkway is to assure Newbury's commercial future in the 21st century.

Chapter 9

The Architectural Heritage

Introduction

This chapter provides a short description of the more interesting buildings of Newbury, but it is not an attempt to cover every one of historic interest. Attention is concentrated on buildings erected before the late 19th century, and is focused on the town centre. First, some outstanding buildings are highlighted for each period; then buildings are described street by street. This section is arranged moving from the north of the town to the south, so that it (or parts of it) can be used for walking tours.

Newbury has lost many good buildings in recent decades, from the Dower House on London Road in the 1950s, to the old King's Head demolished to make way for the Kennet Centre, to Davis' china shop in Northbrook Street replaced by McDonalds, to the tiled front of the Anchor in Northbrook Street … and many more. The more the existing buildings are understood and appreciated, the better protected they will be.

The tiled front of the Anchor pub in Northbrook Street – a sad loss. (Keith Pritchard)

Buildings by period

Medieval
Litten Chapel, Newtown Road.
Very few of the existing buildings in Newbury itself can be shown
conclusively to date back to the medieval period. There is archaeological
and documentary evidence for many medieval buildings, some of which
were rebuilt later (such as St Nicolas' church, established in the 11th
century but completely rebuilt in the Tudor period).

Tudor
49/50 Northbrook Street
24 Northbrook Street – the surviving part of 'Jack of Newbury's House'
102/3 Northbrook Street
St Nicolas' church
The Eight Bells, Bartholomew Street (or early 17th century)
Bartholomew Manor, Argyle Road
Shaw House

17th Century
Manor House, London Road
The Monument, Northbrook Street
Camp Hopson, Northbrook Street
Cloth Hall, Wharf Street
Coxedd's Almshouses, West Mills
Peace's Almshouses, West Mills
Weavers' Cottages, West Mills
49/50 Cheap Street
St Bartholomew's Hospital/Almshouses, Argyle Road

18th Century
Goldwell, Old Bath Road
Chestnuts, Old Bath Road
St Mary's House, London Road
York House/ Thames Court, Broadway
42 Northbrook Street
91/92 Northbrook Street
Newbury Bridge
5 Wharf Street
The Granary
St Nicolas House, West Mills

(Above) *Northbrook Street from the bridge, 1851*

(Below) *Northbrook Street from the bridge, 2011, some 160 years on.*

28 Bartholomew Street
63 Cheap Street

19th Century
22 Oxford Road
National Westminster Bank, Market Place
Corn Exchange, Market Place
Town Hall, Market Place
St Nicolas' School/ National schools, Enborne Road

Buildings in the Town, street by street
OLD BATH ROAD

Starting near the junction with Speen Lane, Castle House (46 and 48, with no. 50) is on the site of the Castle Inn, a famous coaching establishment in the 18th and 19th centuries, whose prominent visitors included King George IV. This was considerably altered in the 19th century, when the main building was converted into three houses. No serious research has been done to establish how much remains of the Castle Inn in and around the existing buildings.

The stone pillar or obelisk at the junction of Speen Lane came from the Broadway, where the Clock Tower now stands (see below).

The Lawn (no. 24, Kier Moss) has an 18th-century front, five windows wide. This is the right-hand section of the building, with a porch and fanlight above the door, and was for many years the home of Kleinwort Benson. There is an extension to the left, and modern extensions further left and to the rear, now occupied by Micro Focus.

Goldwell (no. 5, Graphico) is said to have been built about 1740, although it was alterations in the 19th century which are responsible for the appearance of the top floor. The house contains a fine staircase in late 17th-century style, and originally sat in extensive gardens now partly occupied by a housing estate and recreation land linked to Northcroft. The house has been used as offices for more than 30 years, but for about a century it was the home of the Page family. They played a prominent role in the town in the 18th and early 19th century, and in 1768 Francis Page purchased all the shares of the Kennet Navigation (see Chapter 5) to become the sole owner.

Speen Court (or Maplespeen Court, now apartments) is a mid to late 18th-century house of red and grey brick, with brick pilasters and a moulded cornice. It was originally built with two storeys, and a third has been added above the cornice. The large bow window to the west was added in the early 19th century.

The Chestnuts (no. 2, Ross Brooke) is a fine early Georgian house. The date 1720 is recorded on the roof, but the building is more in the earlier Queen Anne-style. It is also of red and grey brick, with two storeys, plus attic rooms and cellars. The south front has a pediment and there are decorative details in the brickwork, while the window heads are of rubbed brick with very narrow joints.

OXFORD ROAD

Opposite the entrance to Waitrose, Wessex House (no. 22, formerly The Shrubbery) is an early 19th-century, Regency-style house, now offices. Across the front is an iron trellis veranda, shading the entrance and two sets of French windows on the ground floor. It has two storeys, and the front has Ionic pilasters rising the whole height to a moulded cornice.

OXFORD STREET

On the south side is the High House (no. 37), which stands out as a tall building of three floors and a basement, and was built in the middle to late 18th century. There are shallow brick arches to the first floor, into which the windows are set (a feature which appears in 18th-century Newbury buildings, spreading to smaller houses in the early 19th century). Columns flank the doorway, with a portico above. There is a fanlight over the door itself, which stands above a short flight of steps.

Queen Anne House (no. 35, Hopwood Ash and First Mortgage Co.). This building may date from the 17th century (i.e. earlier than Queen Anne) and has an extra floor added above the original moulded brick eaves cornice. For some years up to the 1980s the building was divided into two houses, but the right-hand front door has been restored as a window. The entrance is unusually high above the pavement, with much of the basement above ground level.

Albion House (no. 27) is a mid-18th-century building, five bays wide, with the bay on each side being set slightly back. The shape of the rubbed brick across the top of the windows differs on each floor, and a feature has been made of the tall central window of the first floor. Those on the ground floor have large keystones linked to the horizontal string course, all painted white. The house was built by Jonathan Hicks, although the slate roof with its deep eaves is an early 19th-century replacement. In the late 19th and early 20th centuries, this was home to auctioneer and surveyor, A. W. Neate.

On the opposite side, the Bacon Arms (no. 10) was one of Newbury's many coaching inns, as Oxford Street formed part of the Bath Road. On the outside it is a late 18th-century building, but timber beams inside indicate an earlier origin. The arched entrance used by coaches to reach the inn yard is still visible but now forms the hotel's entrance lobby. It was still open in 1984 when the Bacon Arms was used for the 200th anniversary celebration of the first mail-coach run, along the Bath Road. Until the 1820s, it was known as the Maidenhead Inn. Its present name comes from Mr Anthony Bacon, an extremely rich individual who built Elcot Park.

The Chequers (nos. 6–8) has existed for hundreds of years, but not in its present form. It was one of a number of buildings along the north side of Oxford Street, but has spread out to absorb others. The buildings which make up the present hotel were extensively altered in the 19th and early 20th centuries. The Chequers appears by name in a document of 1757, but there are suggestions that it goes back much further.

No. 4 (SW & Company) is an 18th-century, red-brick house, the ground floor faced with stucco in the 19th century to imitate a stone building. A carriageway alongside gives access to the yard and although strictly there is no right of way, it gives an impression of the appearance of the old coach yards. The buildings on the east side of the yard (behind the Gurkha Chef) are the remains of Adnams Brewery or the Speenhamland Brewery, established in 1802, though it had been a brewery before then. The rear building is timber-framed and likely to date from the early 18th century at least. One of the buildings on the west side is said to be part of a 17th-century malthouse.

BROADWAY
In the centre of the Broadway is the Clock Tower (or Clock House) of 1929. On the same spot, in 1828, a stone pillar was erected with a gas lamp on top. The pillar, provided by Frederick Page of nearby Goldwell (supported by public subscription), is now at the junction of the Old Bath Road and Speen Lane.

In 1889 this was replaced by an elaborate iron lamp-post and clock, erected to mark Queen Victoria's Jubilee in 1887. This was generally known as the 'Jubilee Clock'. The attached lamps were later removed and replaced by free-standing lamps, and many pictures show it with the 'Russian gun' and a horse trough.

In 1929 the Jubilee Clock was replaced by the Clock Tower or Clock House, designed by C. R. Rowland Clark and built by Hitchmans of Speenhamland. The money for this was donated by Mr James Henry Godding of Ellerslie, London Road. The designs and inscription refer to it as the 'Clock House', but to local people it quickly became the Clock Tower, and that is how it has generally been known.

Nos. 26 and 24 (Gurkha Chef and the former Threshers) were once the Bear Inn. This was another coaching inn, with a more ancient history although the present frontage is 18th-century. A reference to 'Le Beare' at Speenhamland appears in a document of 1631. It was reportedly to the Bear that the bodies of Lord Falkland, Lord Carnarvon, and Lord Sunderland were brought after the First Battle of Newbury, from the old Guildhall in the Market Place, before being taken away for burial elsewhere. Visitors claimed include Oliver Cromwell, Charles II, James II, and William of Orange. The inn also gained a reputation for cock-fighting. There are extensive cellars.

Thames Court (nos. 20 and 22, formerly York House) and the three buildings to the east formed the famous George and Pelican Inn. Thames Court is one of Newbury's outstanding buildings, looking straight down the Broadway and Northbrook Street, although the Clock Tower now obscures the view in the opposite direction. It was originally the George Inn, and the buildings to the right were the Pelican, until they merged. It was a busy inn with many prominent visitors, including royalty and statesmen, with King George III, Admiral Lord Nelson and Charles Dickens among them. There were extensive stables at the rear, with the entrance near the present zebra crossing, running back to Pelican Lane. Thames Court/York House probably dates from the early 18th century. During the 20th century the ground floor was converted to a bank and a shop, but it was restored in the 1980s, when the two doorways were installed. It was at the George and Pelican that magistrates agreed the Speenhamland System of poor relief in 1795 (see Chapter 5). At one time York House was home to James H. Money, the architect who designed the Town Hall.

On the east side of the Broadway is the King's Coffee House (Hethertons), which has a 19th-century front but may date from the 17th century.

Next to the Coffee House the Broadway narrows. This marks the old boundary between the parishes of Newbury and Speen; and as Speenhamland was part of Speen, it also marks the boundary between Speenhamland and Newbury. The boundary was formed by the Northbrook (sometimes called Speenhamland Water), a branch of the River Kennet that flowed across Northcroft and then through The Marsh/Victoria Park before rejoining the main channel. Jutting out into the road on the Northbrook Street side was the George and Dragon pub.

LONDON ROAD

Along the north side, the Cross Keys (no. 8) was a well-known coaching inn, and is the subject for a drawing of a coaching supper by Cruikshank. However, the current building is a 19th-century replacement.

Past the junction with Pelican Lane is the Manor House (no. 34, also known as Speenhamland Manor). At its heart, this building is 17th-century or earlier, but was re-fronted in the 18th century. During Queen Victoria's reign, it was home to local surgeon and historian Dr Silas Palmer (1815–1875), one of the founders of Newbury District Field Club. Its staircase has been described as 17th-century, but the porch is a relatively modern addition.

St Mary's House, with its battlements, is an architectural treasure (no. 40, ProVision, Two Nine O Five, and more). The lack of certainty about its origins says much about the poverty of research into Newbury's buildings. The frontage was probably added about 1765–70, and is in the 'Gothick' style, which was produced as part of a revival of interest in the Middle Ages. The stonework around the doorway and windows helps to create its distinct character. The architect was probably John Chute of The Vyne, near Basingstoke (now a National Trust property). Chute designed Donnington Grove for James Pettit Andrews, and St Mary's House is in a similar style. Chute was strongly connected with Horace Walpole, whose Strawberry Hill at Twickenham is also a 'Gothick' building. Andrews had married into the Penrose family, and his in-laws are associated with St Mary's House. At the end of the First World War it became the vicarage for St Mary's church (Speenhamland, since demolished), which was further along London Road, and that is how it acquired its current name. In recent years it has been used as a business centre, with suites of offices for rent.

Clarendon House (no. 44, West Berkshire Funeral Directors) was built in the 1750s, as an extension to the King's Arms Inn, another coaching inn.

St Mary's House, 40 London Road, has a fine 18th-century front.

This imposing building, later renamed the Dower House and for many years an antiques centre, was demolished in 1956.

Near the Robin Hood roundabout is St Joseph's church, a Roman Catholic church built in 1927–8 in a style which has been described as Early Christian, Byzantine and Italian Romanesque. Next door is the smaller, plainer church of 1864.

NORTHBROOK STREET
Building numbers start at Newbury Bridge, run up towards the Clock Tower, and then back down the other side. However, the buildings have been arranged here as a walk down from the Clock Tower end, towards Newbury Bridge.

50 Northbrook Street (Winknorth, Bradley & Willows, Mission Hair) was the premises of one of Newbury's leading grocers or 'provision merchants', J. Webb & Sons, for many years. In the late 1980s the building was stripped down to its frame and restored, with its curves straightened out. It was then clear that it had originally been two or more buildings, made to look like one building by the tiling on the front. In the 17th and 18th centuries, tile-hung walls, as well as roofs were a common feature of buildings in Newbury area, with the tiles made locally.

Behind 50 Northbrook Street and visible from Park Street is a building

A half-timbered building dating back to around 1500 was revealed in 1988, as part of the redevelopment of 49–50 Northbrook Street. The demolition of what had been described as an 'old barn' was refused.

The restored 'old barn', with its projecting first-floor jetty, was saved and refurbished.

of c1500. This was destined for demolition in 1988 when 50 Northbrook Street was refurbished. Berkshire County Council's conservation specialist recognised its importance, and it was restored as well. It is a rare survival in this area of a timber-framed late medieval/Tudor town dwelling. Although it is relatively plain and much smaller than Jack of Newbury's house, it would have been the home of a prosperous man.

The Monument Inn (no. 57) is a 17th-century building with tile-hung gables. Documents survive showing that in 1677 this building consisted of two cottages. Shortly afterwards it became the Monument, named after the Monument to the Great Fire of London, which was built 1671–77. Timber-framing inside and the style of the roof confirm that it was built in the 17th century, or earlier. The earliest known reference to the Monument as a pub is in 1735, a reference to property 'in possession of him the said Thomas Field situate in Northbrook Street in Newberry aforesaid known by the sign of the Monument …'

The Methodist church was built in 1837–8, at the beginning of Queen Victoria's reign. It stands back from the street, and was originally hidden from the passer-by; the cottage in front was demolished in the 19th century, opening up the present view. Originally Wesleyan Methodist (as opposed to the Primitive Methodists in Bartholomew Street), the church was restored in the 1980s after a successful fund-raising appeal.

No. 59 (Hampton's International and Framemakers) was Newbury Picture Palace, Newbury's second cinema, which opened more than a century ago. The slightly overhanging upper floor which housed the projection equipment can still be seen.

Opposite, Specsavers (no. 42) is an unusual highly-decorated building. Its date, 1724, appears on the first floor, to the right, with an entangled set of initials to balance it on the left. All the first-floor window arches have carved keystones, and the first floor is decorated on each site with a pair of Corinthian pilasters, and in the centre with two smaller pairs of Ionic pilasters. Originally four small statues stood on the edge of the roof, and they were still there in the mid-1930s. In the late 19th century this was home to local photographer, Thomas Howe, followed in the early 20th century by another photographer, J.W. Righton, who produced many postcards of local views. The style of the building is rare, and one writer suggests that it was built by someone who had visited or who had come from the Netherlands in the early 18th century, during Marlborough's wars.

Vodafone (no. 77) is an early 19th-century building, with shallow brick arches on the first floor.

Just off Northbrook Street, facing into Marsh Lane, is the Tudor gable of Jack of Newbury's House (Monsoon, no. 24). This is just a fragment of the original building, which was arranged around courtyards, and ran from the corner of Marsh Lane at least as far towards the bridge as Jack Street, stretching back towards the Marsh (Victoria Park). The main part of this building became the Jack Hotel, which closed in the 1930s and was demolished to be replaced by Marks & Spencer. The total street frontage was at least 29m (96 ft). In size alone it stands out as a significant house for its time. It is mentioned about 1550 as the home of John Winchcombe (c1489–1557), or Jack of Newbury, on the east side of Northbrook Street. Winchcombe's will gives details of many rooms including the hall, which was wood-panelled with tapestries hanging from the walls. Some of the carved panels have survived, and are now at Sudeley Castle in Gloucestershire, or incorporated into a sideboard belonging to West Berkshire Museum. Others have been engraved or photographed, but are now missing. The merchant's mark of John Winchcombe appears on some of these. The full house contained at least nine bedrooms, mainly for the Winchcombe family and their servants. Winchcombe's bedroom had a four-poster bed and wall-hangings, with four red and green curtains at the windows. A brewhouse and bakehouse are mentioned. This was the house which received a grand visit from the future Protector Somerset (Edward Seymour) in September 1537, when he gave money to those carding wool for Winchcombe. It was also the subject of a legendary visit from King Henry VIII and his Queen.

The surviving part of the building in Marsh Lane jetties out at the first and second floor level. It would have done the same into Northbrook Street, but this part has been altered. On the ground floor, bricks fill in the space closest to Northbrook Street, so that the front lines up with the first floor. On the second floor, the end of the roof has been sawn off. These changes were made in the Georgian period to modernise the front of the building. On the north side in Marsh Lane are vertical timbers about 20 cm (8 ins) apart, in a style known as close-studding. The amount of wood used was a form of ostentation, a display of wealth. Exterior carvings survive: a decorated wooden beam or bressumer marks the jetty between ground and first floor, the oriel window is carried on carved brackets, and there is a decorative bargeboard. At the top of the first floor on the east side is the beginning of a pendant with the end missing, which would have been matched by another at the Northbrook Street end.

A recent survey of this part of the building suggested it was built in the late 15th or early 16th century. It was originally an open hall, with the ground floor and the second floor in one high room, and with the moulded decoration on the roof-beams visible to those below; but has been altered on several occasions since.

Above the shop fronts at nos. 91 and 92 Northbrook Street (Vision Express and First Choice) can be seen an imposing 18th-century house. It is seven windows wide and three storeys high, decorated with eight tall pilasters which pass through the cornice to support the parapet. Although the date 1774 appeared on a rainwater head, it was built about 1730 or 1740, probably for a member of the Head family. Laurence Head the Younger (d. 1774), Laurence Head the Elder (d. 1756), and Joseph Head (d. c1712) were all Mayors of Newbury. The house, like several in the town centre, has been attributed to James Clarke of Newbury, who built Newbury Bridge.

Camp Hopson (nos. 10–11), with its twin-gabled roof, is a 17th-century house of national significance. It was built for George Cowslade, 'haberdasher of hatts', and is dated 1663 on the points of the roof. Cowslade purchased the site in 1658, when it housed the George Inn, and built his grand new house in its place. In 1663, just three years after the restoration, when Cowslade was Mayor of Newbury, he received King Charles II when he was touring the Civil War battlefields. The exterior features Doric and Ionic pilasters, and is a very early example of rubbed brickwork. Inside is a good staircase with its original ceiling, decorated by an egg-and-tongue cornice with a cherub at its centre. When Camp Hopson opened its doors in May 1921, it occupied nos. 6–14 Northbrook Street, including everything from HSBC to River Island, plus two-thirds of Wilkinsons (formerly Woolworths) (see Chapter 7).

On either side of nos. 10–11, River Island (no 12), and no. 9 (still Camp Hopson) both have 18th-century fronts, the latter with 'WB 1790' on a rainwater head (the year after the outbreak of the French Revolution).

Curry's Digital (no. 94) is opposite; its front is 18th- and 19th-century, but the building was altered from a 17th-century house.

The old Tudor Cafe (nos. 102 and 103, now Accessorize and Clarks) is on the west side of the street, between Northcroft Lane and Newbury Bridge. This is an area in which various Tudor clothiers had property: Thomas Bedford, John Winchcombe II, Brian Chamberlain and Philip

The façade of Camp Hopson's department store carries a date of 1663.

Kistell, and possibly Thomas Dolman. The references include a building called the Hart or White Hart, which was on this site or perhaps next to it. For example, a lease of 1564 to clothier Brian Chamberlain refers to a 'tenement in which he dwelleth in Northbroke Street on the West side of the same street sometime called the sign of the Harte.' The Tudor Cafe has never been properly surveyed, but its structure has been described as Elizabethan and the timbers inside suggest a 16th- or 17th-century date, with extensive later alterations. The Tudor Cafe itself was something of a local institution, run by Jack Hole and his wife from the 1930s until its closure in 1973. Jack Hole was a Mayor of Newbury and a photographer, and was awarded the Freedom of Newbury.

NORTHCROFT LANE
On the south side is a continuation of timber-framed buildings which were associated with the former Tudor Cafe, though now incorporated in the Lock, Stock and Barrel pub. On the north side is a former almshouse of 1821 (no. 4), which an inscription reveals was endowed by John Childs, a sail-cloth maker.

Also in Northcroft Lane is a building best known in recent years as the Arts

Workshop, although for nearly a century it was Newbury's Temperance Hall. The front of the building was added in the 19th century, but the rest is earlier. Its origins are unclear, but it has timbers which suggest that it goes back to the medieval period. Work on converting it into a Temperance Hall began in May 1875, with the laying of stones carrying Temperance slogans such as 'The drunkard shall come to poverty' (the worn remains of which are still visible on the front of the building). The Temperance Hall was opened on 17 August 1875 and until the First World War it was at the centre of a thriving local movement. In 1979 it was converted into the Arts Workshop, which continued until 1998. It is now occupied by Little Bears Day Nursery.

Next door is the Salvation Army Hall, a highly-decorated Victorian building of 1893, which uses a striking combination of flint, terracotta and moulded brick.

BRIDGE STREET
Newbury Bridge was built in 1769–72 (see Chapter 5). The four buildings incorporating the bridge's decorative shelters are West Cornwall Pasty Company and Newbury Building Society in Northbrook Street, with Griffins and Britannia Building Society in Bridge Street. The first three of these buildings are mid to late18th-century. The one housing the West Cornwall Pasty Company, with its shallow rounded brick arches (previous occupants including Town Bookseller and Liddiards butchers), had an ornate iron balcony across its front until the 20th century. On the south-east corner of the bridge (no. 4, formerly Cotton Traders, and once Forrest Stores), a mid-18th-century building, has a three-sided bay which once came down to street level. The central windows are 18th-century 'gothick'.

Lloyds Bank (nos. 3–5) is on the site of the old Globe Inn. This was an important inn established in the 17th century or earlier, which hosted local events such as public meetings for turnpike trusts and agricultural enclosures. It closed about 1870 and in 1879 it was purchased by Slocock, Bunny, Matthews and Southby, who traded as the Old Bank (founded 1791). In 1895 this was sold to Capital and Counties Bank who were absorbed into Lloyds Bank in 1918, and it has remained in the same hands since. The walled garden on the island next to Newbury Lock is known as the Globe Garden and was associated with the inn.

MANSION HOUSE STREET
Mansion House Street takes its name from the now-demolished Mansion House, a substantial brick building built about 1742 by James Clarke of

2

3

Newbury, who was responsible for several important buildings in the town and for Newbury Bridge. It was demolished in 1908–9 in order to widen the road, and was replaced by the 'municipal offices', an almost seamless extension of the Town Hall. This is dated 1910 and carries a version of Newbury Castle as the Borough's symbol. It also sports a notice declaring: 'The use of Traction Engines in Mansion House Street is Prohibited.'

MARKET PLACE

On the north side, the buildings of restaurants ASK and Brasserie Gerard (nos. 34 and 32) date from the mid to late 18th century. They were once both part of Beynons (draper & clothier), which in spite of the sign at roof level, moved here in 1894; the sign was changed from Burgess (the previous occupier) to Beynon only after 1903.

NatWest (no. 30) is in an imposing building on the north side of the Market Place. It was erected in 1864, and has a fairly subtle decoration which shows up well when floodlit. It was designed by J. Chancellor, in a style described as 'Italian Gothic'. It was built for the London and County Bank, and has been used by the same firm throughout its history, under a variety of names. In 1909 the London and County merged with the London and Westminster, and eventually became the Westminster Bank. This later merged in turn to form the National Westminster Bank, which began trading at the beginning of 1970.

The Old Waggon and Horses (no. 26) is one of Newbury's old pubs, and features in a list of premises in the town in 1761, when the landlord was Henry Hoskins. Parts of the building date from the 17th century, and the appearance of the front has changed little since early in the 19th century.

On the east, the White Hart (no. 24, on the corner of Wharf Road, now solicitors Gardner Leader), was a coaching inn. It was probably established in the 16th or 17th century, but rebuilt in the early 19th century, and in recent years its interior has seen major alterations. In 1752 the White Hart started advertising 'Flying Coaches' from Newbury to London, fast enough to get passengers to their destination the same day. The entrance to the coaching yard was next to the Cloth Hall, and the yard became the garage when cars arrived. The portico which is now attached to The Chantry in West Mills is said to come from this building.

The Hatchet (no. 12) is another old Newbury pub, included on the 1761 list, when the landlord was Joseph Baster. It used its position in the Market

Place well, in 1849 being listed as the base for cart carriers to Abingdon, Aldermaston, Alton, Alresford, Basingstoke, St Mary Bourne, Faringdon, Farnham, Great Shefford, Oxford and Wantage. In recent years it temporarily changed its name to the Berkshire Tavern, but changed back again after it was acquired by J.D. Wetherspoon, and was restored and refurbished before re-opening as the Hatchet in July 2011.

The Corn Exchange (no. 10) was designed by J.S. Dodd of Reading and was built 1861–2 as a market for corn, in line with similar buildings at Wallingford and Devizes. It opened in June 1862. Newbury Castle (the symbol of the Borough of Newbury) appears in relief over the main entrance. The Corn Exchange has been used for a wide range of roles and played host to many local clubs and societies. It closed in 1988 and in the early 1990s was extensively remodelled by Newbury District Council as an arts centre, re-opening in September 1993.

The Queens Hotel (no. 8) has a 19th-century frontage, but parts are older. Before about 1880 it was known as the Three Tuns, and it is under that name that it appears in the 1761 list, with the landlord as William Dallison.

On the west, the Strada building (the former Daniels department store, nos. 21–25), to the left of the entrance to the Arcade, is early 19th century in appearance. Inside, parts go back much earlier, possibly to the 17th century. During renovation in the 1960s a lead plaque was found bearing the date 1681, which was mounted on the outside of the building, between the first and second floor, where it can still be seen.

The Town Hall was built in 1876–8, with the tower heightened in 1881 to add the clock, which was part of the original design. The architect was Mr James H. Money, brother to Newbury historian Walter Money, and the design appears heavily influenced by Alfred Waterhouse's Reading Town Hall, built 1872–6. Newbury Town Hall was opened in May 1878 by the Earl of Carnarvon, who described it as 'handsome and most satisfactory', and 'well worthy of the town of Newbury.' It was extended into Mansion House Street in 1910 (see above).

WHARF STREET AND THE WHARF

The Hog's Head (or Hogshead, nos. 1–3) was for many years the premises of auctioneers Day, Shergold and Herbert, with large sale rooms to the rear. The frontage is 19th-century, but as with so many Newbury buildings, parts of the structure are earlier.

Number 5 is a striking building of the early/mid 18th century, with an imposing façade. This has been attributed to James Clarke of Newbury, who built Newbury Bridge and has long merited some serious research. Now it is used by Gardner Leader solicitors, who also have the White Hart in the Market Place.

The Cloth Hall (south side) was built in the 17th century thanks to a bequest from John Kendrick, which was also responsible for the original Oracle in Reading. Both buildings were intended as job-creation schemes, sometimes called 'workhouses' before the word became associated with the more grim Victorian institutions and Oliver Twist. The Cloth Hall was built in 1626–7 as one wing of a three-wing building arranged around a courtyard; a courtyard which is now represented by the line of Wharf Street. Faces appear in the brackets supporting the first floor. At the beginning of the 20th century it was converted to become Newbury Museum (see Chapter 7), opening in October 1904. The museum, now West Berkshire Museum, is currently closed pending plans for renovation. The weather vane is a replica of the weather vane on the old Guildhall in the Market Place, demolished in the 1820s. Linked to the Cloth Hall and also part of the museum is an extension of 1934, paid for largely by Newbury District Field Club in memory of historian Walter Money. The terracotta badge of Newbury Castle on the front came from the Queen Victoria statue which stood in the Market Place (elements of which are now in Victoria Park).

On the opposite side of the road, Wharf House and Kendrick House have suffered from changing names. Facing across the Wharf, at right angles to the Granary, is Wharf House, for some time home of the Dolton family. This building (long known as Kendrick House) is a good mid-18th-century building, altered in the early 19th century, and the front doorway with its fanlight dates from around this period. It is now occupied by Charles Hoile, solicitors, who moved out of Park Way to make way for the shopping development. The name Kendrick House now applies to the 20th-century building which houses ICN Computers and until recently Vinyl Revival, with flats and offices above.

The Granary (also called the Corn Stores) is a long and picturesque building with heavy timbers, much of it used by the museum. The ground floor is sheltered by the overhanging gallery which is approached by a double central staircase. This originally gave access to the individual storerooms of the first floor, and is protected by an extension of the tiled roof. The ground floor also consisted of storerooms, with the windows added in the 1930s. The Granary is thought to have been built as part of the creation of the Kennet Navigation (from the Act in 1715 to opening in 1723), which turned Newbury into a significant inland port (see Chapter 5). The Granary provided stores alongside a canal basin where barges and later narrow boats were loaded and unloaded. However, there has been some evidence to suggest a 17th-century date, and (uniquely for Newbury) English Heritage and its predecessors have swung from a 17th-century date to 18th-century and back again, while recent work indicates that this should return once more to an 18th-century date.

The origins of the stone building near the Kennet (used by the Kennet and Avon Canal Trust) are unclear, and the suggestion is that it was built after the opening of the Kennet and Avon Canal in 1810, with stone brought from Bath. However, it is difficult to see why a relatively expensive material should be used for what is really a low-status building, rather than using local materials. There are tales that it was built with stone from Newbury Castle, or from Donnington Castle, both of which were destroyed long before this was built. To date the stone itself has not been analysed.

On the far side of the Wharf is Newbury Library, which was designed by Sutton, Griffin & Morgan and opened in 2000.

CHEAP STREET
On the east side is the post office (no. 40) which opened in 1896, built in a Victorian Tudor-style.

Opposite, the Catherine Wheel (no. 35) has a 19th-century frontage with Tudor-style chimneys.

Charles Clinkard and Marshalls (nos. 33 & 34) was a 17th-century building, rebuilt with the roof raised one storey higher. The roof has bargeboards and pendants which appear to be faithful copies of the original. They bear the date 1679 and the initials 'SAM', for Samuel and Ann Merriman.

Downer & Co., estate agents, (no. 44) inhabit an exuberant late Victorian building, probably of 1870–80. It is built of grey brick with terracotta shafts dividing the first floor windows, which have terracotta keystones.

The A2B Taxi Booking Office and Harris Hair (nos. 49–50) occupy a 17th-century building which has some features in common with the Monument pub in Northbrook Street, and (although more modest), with the 1663 part of Camp Hopson. For years the date 1637 was painted on the front of this building, and that is a possible date for its construction – before the start of the Civil War. It has been extended to the south, over the entrance to Dothan Place: its houses long gone, but the name still visible.

The former Newbury Library, which opened in 1906, became redundant when the new library opened on The Wharf on 2000. It is now occupied by the restaurant chain, Prezzo.

On the west side of the road Mills & Bann, solicitors, (no. 8) was occupied by Neates, estate agents, from the First World War to the 1980s, when the firm merged with Dreweatts. Under its painted surface it has a late 18th-century variegated brick frontage.

On the other side of the entrance to the Baptist church (built 1939–40) is the former shop and warehouse of Midwinters, seed merchant (no. 7, West Berkshire Training Consortium). This is a late Victorian industrial building, with cast-iron window frames to the side.

Opposite, no. 63 was built in 1796 and is said to have been built by T. Green. The Doric doorway has a semi-circular fanlight. The building's full-height curved bay windows, associated with the Regency period, are an unusual style in Newbury.

WEST MILLS
St Nicolas' House (no. 3, Youth Department of St Nicolas' church) is an important mid-18th-century building, another from this period attributed to or in the style of James Clarke of Newbury. The elaborate doorway has a semi-circular fanlight and a hood supported by brackets displaying cherubs' heads. The house is of grey brick with red-brick dressings, and the windows have semi-elliptical heads of rubbed brick, the first floor with 'apron' decorations below. Inside is a contemporary staircase with three designs of baluster to each step. Attached to St Nicolas House is The Chantry, an 18th-century building, with a fine 18th-century porch, reputed to have be moved from the White Hart in the Market Place.

The former Town Mills, on a site which goes back to the 11th century or earlier, have been replaced by blocks of modern flats.

The former Hunt Almshouses (no. 11) are set end-on to the road. They were built in 1817 and have 'gothick' detail to the windows.

Nos. 15/16 (part of Horsey Lightly solicitors) are the former Coxedd's Almshouses, with their steeply-sloping roof. These were established in the late 17th century by the will of Francis Coxedd or Coxhead (1690) and consist of two small cottages with a shared entrance porch. They are best known in recent years as an antiques shop.

Next but one is the former Pearce's Almshouses (no. 17, west side, and no. 18), founded in 1672, but using a building which already existed. The ground floor wall was originally further back, leaving the timber-framed first floor to jetty forward. The sash windows with dripmoulds are 18th-century. A 17th-century wooden carving from above the left doorway is now in Enborne Road, moved when replacement almshouses were established in the 1880s.

The Club House (no. 22) is an early 18th-century house on the corner of Kennet Road. Built of red brick it has a moulded string course at first floor level and a moulded eaves cornice, but the doorway has been altered. It displays a fire insurance mark for Sun Insurance Policy No. 332180, dated 30 October 1773 (the year of the 'Boston Tea Party').

Across Kennet Road is the end of the Weavers Cottages, tile-hung and with a pretty oriel window. In spite of the name, there is little evidence relating to their original use; there are strong cloth industry connections in this area, and in particular with the West Mills opposite, which were Tudor fulling mills. The Weavers Cottages were reportedly built at the beginning of the 17th century, and are timber-framed with brick infilling. Originally seven cottages, they were altered in 1963, converted into two houses. Much of the exterior has been covered with roughcast.

ST NICOLAS' CHURCH
St Nicolas' church was completely rebuilt in the Tudor period (see Chapter 3), with current evidence supporting a construction period from 1520 to 1534. Although so far there is little supporting documentary evidence, the major sponsor appears to have been John Winchcombe (c1489–1557), whose merchant's mark alternates with his father's monogram in the bosses of the nave roof. The building was altered in the Georgian period (when the battlements were removed) and was then altered again by the Victorians (Henry Woodyer, 1858–63, when the battlements were replaced). However, it is still substantially the church built during the reign of King Henry VIII. The stained glass was added in the late 19th century and includes a window to 'Jack of Newbury', dedicated in 1884, which includes

illustrations of carvings discovered in buildings at the rear of the Jack Hotel in the 19th century. The reredos is by Ninian Comper, 1905. Under the tower is a brass to John Smallwood alias Winchcombe (d.1519/20), father of Jack of Newbury, and one of his wives.

The stone entrance gateways to the churchyard from Bartholomew Street were probably built in 1770.

Just inside the West Mills gateway to the churchyard, to the left, is a large flat stone. This is thought to be the 'bench' on which a medieval bow-string maker rolled strings for archers to use on their long bows. It was identified in a shop (at one time the King's Head Inn) close to the Market Place entrance to the Kennet Centre, and was brought to the churchyard when the buildings there were demolished. A bow string maker is recorded as living in that area.

BARTHOLOMEW STREET

The Snooty Fox (no. 148) is a building of 1875 which opened as the Globe, taking the name of the established inn on the corner of West Mills and Bridge Street, which had recently closed. The Snooty Fox incorporates several elements of local traditional building styles: brick-built, with a tiled roof with prominent bargeboards, decorated with tile-hanging, pilasters and an obvious cornice. The Victorian pub survived relatively intact until the 1980s, when there were considerable alterations.

The Bricklayers Arms (recently the Purple Lounge, no. 137) has an early 19th-century first floor, but the ground floor is much altered, with the waggon entrance incorporated within the building. Before it became the Bricklayers it was the Half Moon, and it is under this name that it appears in the 1761 list of Newbury's pubs.

Many of the old buildings north of the junction with Market Street were demolished in the late 1960s and early 1970s to make way for the Kennet Centre. Among them was Herborough House, close to the junction with Market Street, which was the home of Newbury historian Walter Money, later occupied by Nias, and demolished in 1970.

On the opposite side, no. 28 is an early to mid-18th-century house. It has a good doorway with an elliptical fanlight. For several decades in the 19th century it was home to surgeon Dr Stephen Hemsted, and it has provided offices for Charles Lucas and Marshall for more than 30 years.

In Inch's Yard (the name is from the former Inch's drapers), Studio Thai is in a converted 18th-century maltings. Two original mullioned windows (which would have been unglazed) survive, though the two lower ones are replacements. Next to it is a three-storey industrial building, the uprights on the second floor are from sets of wooden louvres which once formed its walls, and two first floor loading doors can be seen, though the brick structure of the building is much altered.

The Dolphin Inn (no. 113) appears to be 17th-century and, at the rear, timber-framing and tile-hung gables can be seen. The front was rebuilt in the late 18th/early 19th centuries and has a very flat elliptical arch of rubbed bricks over the former waggon entrance. This entrance, unlike most others, has not been incorporated into the inn, although there have been alterations. The Dolphin appears under the same name in the 1761 list of Newbury pubs, with John Knight as the landlord.

On the corner of Craven Road is the Coopers' Arms (no. 39), which was re-fronted in the early 19th century, but has 18th- and perhaps 17th-century features inside. The roof timbers are betrayed from the outside by the undulating ridge line, but the clay tiles have all been replaced in recent years. It appears as the Coopers' Arms in the 1761 list of Newbury pubs.

The Eight Bells is a late 16th- or early 17th-century building. It was a pub for many years, and features in the 1761 list of Newbury pubs, when the landlord was Joseph Harding. The windows were changed in the 19th century, and it continued as a pub until November 1961.

On the west side, Phoenix House (no. 50) was the brewer's house for the Phoenix Brewery. This was established in 1842 as Nutley's Brewery, became Finn's Brewery and continued until H. J. Finn & Co. was purchased by Ushers in 1922. Phoenix House looks like a 19th-century building because of the doorcase and large-paned windows, but the building itself is an early to mid-18th-century house. It has served as Newbury Register Office and as council offices. Some of the 19th-century brewery buildings survive to the rear, although altered.

The building immediately north of the railway bridge (no. 61, until recently Saffron Spa, but occupied by Craftsman for many years) was once the Vine Inn, and is thought to date from the 17th century. The early 18th-century cottages to the rear were extensively restored in the 1990s after becoming derelict.

On the other side of the railway bridge was the Black Boys Hotel (nos. 62–63). Its painted sign can still be made out on the front of the building. This is a substantial 18th-century building with a hipped tile roof, which retains much of its character in spite of the ground-floor shop fronts. It closed as the Black Boys in the mid-1950s. The next building, Bartholomew House (no. 64, Hillier & Wilson, formerly Cottrells office supplies), is known to many Newbury residents as Kimber's Corner, from the grocers established there for over 50 years.

Opposite the Black Boys is a small house and shop, now Supernova Cycles (no. 79) which appears to be timber-framed and is likely to date from the 17th century.

NEWTOWN ROAD

Newtown Road begins at the junction with Pound Street, heading towards and across St John's roundabout. On the junction with Pound Street is The Litten (Dunwoody Marketing Communications), with the tall house rebuilt in 1849 as Newbury Grammar School (St Bartholomew's). The flint-walled chapel which extends towards Newtown Road originally served St Bartholomew's Hospital (see Chapter 2). Original stone windows can be seen, but its real glory lies in the carved timber roof trusses inside. The building was abruptly shortened in the 18th century, and the east end has been rebuilt in brick. The chapel was dedicated to St Leonard, patron saint for childbirth and midwives.

On the opposite site of the road and set at right angles to it are Raymonds' Almshouses (nos. 1–12). This range of twelve units has a central pedimented entranceway bearing the painted name 'Raymonds' and the date '1796'. The buildings have been modernized from time to time, introducing several new features. These replaced the original almshouses in Argyle Road, and are known as Lower Raymonds' Almshouses to differentiate them from a later range in Derby Road.

St John's church was completed in 1957, replacing the building destroyed in 1943. It was designed by Mr S.E. Dykes-Bower (architect to Westminster Abbey) who specified locally-made bricks to smaller than usual dimensions, which give the illusion of increased height and space. In 1988, the church was amongst the first post-war buildings in Newbury to be listed as being of architectural interest.

ARGYLE ROAD

On the corner of Pound Street is Bartholomew Close, a group of cottages converted by Dr Essex Wynter to provide nurses' accommodation. Though essentially 17th- or 18th-century, single-storey cottages with attics, they have had substantial renovations; for example there were shop windows in the Argyle Road elevation at the beginning of the 20th century.

Bartholomew Manor (no. 4) has medieval origins and may date from the 14th or 15th centuries, but was transformed into a high-status home in the 16th century. After the First World War it was purchased by Dr Essex Wynter, who made it his home. He researched the history of the building, visiting the archive at St George's Chapel in Windsor, which took over most of the property previously owned by Sandleford Priory. Wynter identified this building as 'Bartilmewes', and gave it is modern name, Bartholomew Manor. 'Bartilmewes' had been leased by John Winchcombe (c1489–1557), and by his son Henry (c1522–1562). Wynter suggested that the 16th-century alterations may have coincided with Henry inheriting the property about 1557. Henry Winchcombe was a clothier in his own right, and is documented as producing the 'New Draperies' in Newbury, as well as the more traditional kersey cloths. In the 1920s Wynter altered and restored the house, but in doing so used genuine Tudor materials from elsewhere, creating difficulties for future architectural historians. The render has been stripped from the front in recent years, exposing the brickwork.

Opposite is St Bartholomew's Hospital (nos. 1–27, odd), also called King John's Almshouses. Although founded in the reign of King John, this building goes back to 1618, with the entrance tower added and other alterations in 1698, and later. The Royal Arms are 18th-century.

The former Raymonds Almshouses (nos. 12–26, even) are thought to have been converted from farm buildings in 1670 by Philip Jemmet, a member of the Brewer's Company (hence the company's arms and an appropriate date and initials above the entrance). The almshouses were further endowed by his son-in-law and daughter, Sir Jonathan and Lady Raymond. In the 1920s Dr Essex Wynter purchased the building and altered it by raising the roof on a timber-framed structure (using old materials) to create a second floor for his nurses' home, completed in 1929.

Opposite the end of Derby Road are the Nurses' Homes (nos. 30–40, even), sometimes mistaken for Tudor buildings but built in 1937 by Dr Essex Wynter for retired nurses of the Middlesex Hospital, London.

Further Reading

Newbury Histories
V.F.M. Garlick, *Newbury Scrapbook*, 1970
Walter Money, *The History of Newbury*, 1887
Walter Money, *The Popular History of Newbury*, 1905 (and reprinted 1972, with foreword by Helen Purvis)
Newbury Buildings Past and Present, 1973.
Helen Purvis, *Talking About Newbury: A Brief History*, 1988
Susan Tolman, *Newbury History and Guide*, 1994
R.B. Tubb, *Newbury Road by Road*, 2011

Photographic Histories
Peter Allen, *Britain in Old Photographs: Newbury*, 1995
Tony Higgott, *Newbury in the 1950s*, 2004
Sue Hopson, *Newbury: A Photographic Record 1850–1935*, 1983
Sue Hopson, *Newbury Then and Now*, 1988
Nick Channer, *Newbury Living Memories*, 2004

Local Topics
Berkshire Archaeological Journal, published regularly for over a century, including articles on a wide range of topics of local interest (not just archaeology); available online
Frances M. Berry, *A Newbury Family*, 1996 (and other works by the same author)
Joan Booker, *A Newbury Childhood*, 1982
David H. Brazier, *A History of the Newbury Baptists*, 2003
Colin Buchanan, *Traffic in Towns* (the Buchanan Report), 1963
Kenneth Clew, *The Kennet and Avon Canal* (several editions)
V.F M. Garlick, *Newbury Charities and Gifts*, 1972
Robert L. Gibbs, *History of St. John's Church and Parish*, Newbury, 1990
Richard Godfrey, *Newbury Borough Police 1836-1875*, 2008
Paul Lacey, *A History of Newbury & District Motor Services Limited 1932 to 1952*, 1987 (and others on motor transport)
Michael Macleod, *Shaw House Unmask'd*, 1999
Walter Money, *Collections for the History of the Parish of Speen*, 1892
W.A.D. Morris, *A History of the Parish of Shaw-cum-Donnington*, 1969

Transactions of Newbury District Field Club, published regularly from 1870 to the present, including articles on a wide range of topics of local interest

Daphne Phillips, *The Great Road to Bath*, 1983

Malcolm Phillips, *Voices of Ormonde House: A history of the early years of Newbury College*, 2011

Brian Philpott, *The Bombing of Newbury*, 1989

Helen Purvis, *St George the Martyr, Wash Common, Newbury: The story of the first 50 Years*, 1983

Paul Ranger, *A Catalogue of Strolling Companies, the ongoing theatre in Newbury*, 1990

St Nicolas Church guides (many authors and editions)

R.B. Tubb, *Greenham Road by Road*, 2004

R.B. Tubb, Speen, Stockcross, Shaw-cum-Donnington Road by Road, 2002

Victoria County History: Berkshire (4 vols, Newbury in vol. iv). In spite of its age, this provides a good framework for aspects of local history including the descent of the manor, and gives documentary references (available online at www.british-history.ac.uk).

West Berkshire Heritage Service – assorted guides on topics of local interest available from the Museum/Tourist Information Centre.

Margaret Wood, *Donnington Castle: Berkshire*, 1964

Battles of Newbury
John Barratt, *The First Battle of Newbury*, 2005

Jon Day, *Gloucester & Newbury 1643*, 2007

Michael McNair-Wilson, *Battle for a Kingdom*, 1993

Walter Money, *The First and Second Battles of Newbury and the Siege of Donnington Castle*, 1881

Keith Roberts, *First Newbury 1643*, 2003

Christopher L. Scott, *The Battles of Newbury*, 2008

Websites
Berkshire Archaeological Society: www.berksarch.co.uk

Berkshire Record Office (Reading): www.berkshirerecordoffice.org.uk

Heritage Gateway: www.westberks.gov.uk/HERonline

Newbury District Field Club: www.ndfc.org.uk

Newbury Society: www.newbury-society.org.uk

Newbury Town Council: www.newbury.gov.uk

Thatcham Historical Society: www.thatchamhistoricalsociety.org.uk

West Berkshire Council: www.westberks.gov.uk

Index